To

_____

A Gift From

_____

"You'll be blown away by Melanie Notkin's expertise on America's cool aunts, who are over-loved yet overlooked by marketers. If you want to gain the hearts and dollars of these kid-loving, high-spending women, *Savvy Auntie* is a must-read."

—Mary Lou Quinlan, CEO of Just Ask a Woman and author of *What She's Not Telling You*

"Here's a Jewish mother's secret: having aunties around to love our kids and give us the support we need is priceless. Melanie's book honors our sisters and friends, and I can't think of anyone more deserving."

—Jill Zarin, star of *The Real Housewives of New York City* and coauthor of *Secrets of a Jewish Mother*

"*Savvy Auntie* is not only hugely informative, it's great fun to read. Give it to all your girlfriends—they'll thank you, and so will all their lucky nieces and nephews. A great gift for anyone who loves kids."

—Melissa Kirsch, author of *The Girl's Guide to Absolutely Everything*

"A joy to read. *Savvy Auntie* is a fun, comprehensive guide that no auntie (of any kind) should be without! We can't wait to buy it for our friends."

—"The Guncles" Bill Horn and Scout Masterson, stars of *Tori & Dean: Home Sweet Hollywood*

"With this savvy guide, Melanie has changed the way we look at women and family in America. She's identified the one thing all women—straight, gay, married, or single— have in common: an unconditional love for the children in our lives. What a gift she's given her auntourage."

—Jenny Stewart, entertainment journalist voted one of Power Up's 10 Amazing Gay Women in Showbiz

# savvy auntie

# savvy auntie

## THE ULTIMATE GUIDE FOR COOL AUNTS, GREAT-AUNTS, GODMOTHERS, AND ALL WOMEN WHO LOVE KIDS

*Melanie Notkin*

WILLIAM MORROW

*An Imprint of HarperCollinsPublishers*

This book contains advice and information relating to health care. It is not intended to replace medical advice and should be used to supplement rather than replace regular care by your doctor. It is recommended that you seek your physician's advice before embarking on any medical program or treatment. All efforts have been made to assure the accuracy of the information contained in this book as of the date of publication. The publisher and the author disclaim liability for any medical outcomes that may occur as a result of applying the methods suggested in this book.

Savvy Auntie® is a registered trademark. The trademarks of the products mentioned in this book are owned by their respective manufacturers, none of whom compensated the author for their mention.

FIRST EDITION

*Designed by Richard Oriolo*

Library of Congress Cataloging-in-Publication Data has been applied for.

ISBN 978-0-06-199997-0

11 12 13 14 15  OV/RRD  10 9 8 7 6 5 4 3 2 1

To the cool aunts, great-aunts, godmothers,

and all the fabulous women who love a child-not-their-own.

Your love is a gift and this book is yours.

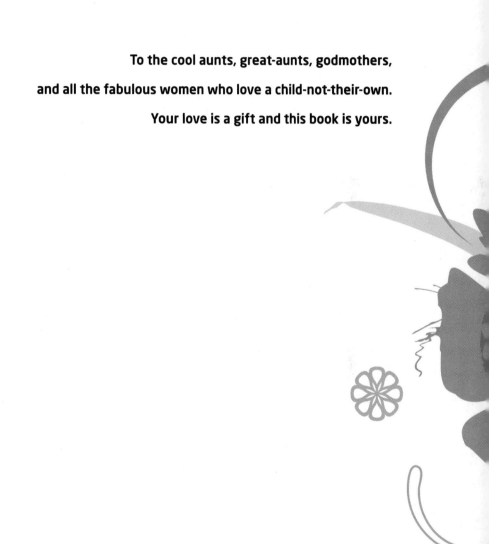

**TO MY MOTHER FOR TEACHING** me the virtues of unconditional love every day of our lives together—virtues that no doubt make me a better auntie. To my father and stepmom who support me unconditionally. To my brother and sister-in-law for making me an Auntie by Relation (ABR), the best gift I could ever receive.

To my firstborn nephew, Z, who changed my life and my world. To my nieces R, M, A, L, and S, you've made my life a beautiful bouquet of flowers. I love you all so much. You are my inspiration.

To Auntie Ethel (ABR), Great-Auntie Sarah (ABR), and Auntie Marilyn (ABC), who are my magnificent auntie-mentors. (Auntie Sarah, I miss you.)

To my friends who have supported me, encouraged me, believed in me, and inspired me.

To Debbie Stier, my original editor at HarperCollins, who discovered me on Twitter as we fell in love with a little girl in Tanzania named @Leah_Albert. Debbie, you've been my champion since the day we met. This book came to be because of your belief in me and Savvy Auntie®. You're an inspiration. To Laurie Chittenden, my editor, who loved, supported, and championed this book before we even met. And to the rest of the incredibly passionate and supportive team at HarperCollins/William Morrow: Seale Ballenger, Kimberly Chocolaad, Trish Daly, Lynn Grady, Jean Marie Kelly, Stephanie Kim, Shawn Nicholls, Kathryn Lee-Ratcliffe, Andrea Rosen, Sharyn Rosenblum, Mary Schuck, Lisa Stokes, Nancy Tan, and, of course, Liate Stehlik. I can't thank you enough for your enthusiastic and heartfelt welcome.

To Rose Maura Lorre, my "Fairy Godwriter." I needed help writing my first book and Rose was there with me all the way, editing my writing, adding her own genius, laughing at all my silly jokes and impressions, and making this an overall extraordinary experience. May I get you some more green tea?

To all the experts on SavvyAuntie.com and those who gave me their time and expertise for the Savvy Auntie book for sharing your wisdom and passion with aunties all over the world. What an honor it's been and continues to be.

To all the people on Twitter and Facebook who have responded with their support, advice, comments, and quotes.

To all the Savvy Auntie members, fans, followers, and friends for being part of this most fabulous tribe of women!

# Contents

## 10 Celebrating You, Auntie! 199

### Appendixes

# An Intro to Savvy Aunthood

1

THE DAY MY NEPHEW WAS born, I took a photo of the sky to remember what the world looked like the day my life changed forever.

When I cradled him in my arms for the first time, I felt the weight of his tiny body. I felt the weight of my devotion to him. *I felt more joy and love than I had ever felt in my life.* In fact, what I felt was a love I'd never known before. A powerful, unconditional, prideful love.

But as the days, weeks, and months passed, I realized that as much as my nephew changed my life, my life actually didn't change that much. I still went to work, on dates, out with my friends. Other than photographs, I had no badge of honor to express my aunthood. And believe me, I

# Hero Auntie!

looked. But in a city as big as New York, all I could find was a little onesie that read IF YOU THINK I'M CUTE, YOU SHOULD SEE MY AUNT.

It started to dawn on me that I was sort of in limbo. Becoming a parent gained a person automatic membership into a huge tribe of fellow parents, with access to all the advice and expertise he or she might seek. Yet there I was, a savvy senior executive at a global cosmetics company, living a very cosmopolitan life but having hardly the first clue about being an aunt. In fact, all I really did have was a very strong desire not to screw up this whole auntie-ing responsibility. I had no books written for me to read, no online resources, no tribe. Where was my tribe?

It took me a while to answer that question, but in the summer of 2008, I finally did. I launched SavvyAuntie.com. And with it, our tribe.

I thought, if I felt this way and my friends felt this way—and if nearly 50 percent of the adult females in the United States are nonmoms (which is only the first of several surprising statistics you will read in this book)—then it's possible that a large part of the American community is being neglected. This meant that there were aunties out there like me who didn't even know there were other aunties out there like them.

As I began to connect with this community (and with the parents of their nieces and nephews), I started to see just how important a role an auntie plays in what I've come to call the American Family Village. An auntie is a woman who makes sacrifices, whether that means taking on extra work during another woman's maternity leave or contributing part of her income toward a niece's or nephew's education. And while this woman may be highly valued within her immediate family and circle of friends, in the greater, collective sense, she was woefully underrepresented and underappreciated.

Even in our modern, politically correct society, the auntie—when she is a woman without children of her own, as nearly half of all American women are—is often called selfish, pathetic, or made to feel "less than." How can this woman, when everything she does for a child-not-her-own is a generous gift, ever be called selfish? How can this woman, who is every other woman in the United States, be an oddball?

These questions remind me of what Helen Gurley Brown set out to resolve with her revolutionary 1962 book *Sex and the Single Girl*. "Nobody was championing [single women]," Brown said in a 1967 interview. "Volumes had been written about this creature, but they all treated the single girl like a scarlet-fever victim, a misfit, and . . . you can't really categorize one-third of the female population [a figure that's only grown since then] as misfits."

Like Ms. Gurley Brown, I set out to start a movement! After all, we're talking about a pretty influential segment of women, culturally, politically, and financially. I dubbed this segment PANK®: Professional Aunt No Kids.

## The PANK Demographic

The U.S. Census Report "Fertility of American Women: 2008" states that 45.7 percent of women through the age of forty-four do not have children, and even fewer women are having children than in 2006 (45.1 percent). In fact, according to the report, "childlessness has been increasing steadily since 1976 when 35 percent of women in the childbearing ages were childless."

"Women without children" data, broken down by age range:

15 to 19 years: 93.7% ❋ 20 to 24 years: 70.6% ❋ 25 to 29 years: 46.2%

30 to 34 years: 26.8% ❋ 35 to 39 years: 19.4% ❋ 40 to 44 years: 17.8%

These data do not include women age forty-five and older, so I can confidently make the assumption that nearly 50 percent of American women are childless, as few women age forty-five and older have children for the first time.

## Money in the PANK!

Whether single, married, or partnered, we PANKs pack a powerful punch. Here are some key stats that demonstrate the power of the PANKs' collective purse.

According to the 2000 U.S. Census, 50 percent of single women own their own homes. They're also the fastest-growing segment of new home buyers, second home buyers, car purchasers, new investors, and travelers. (Who hasn't dreamed of taking the nieces and nephews on their first trip to Disney World?)

Twenty-seven percent of American households are headed by women, a fourfold increase since 1950.

Of American women who draw annual incomes of $100,000 or more, nearly half don't have children. In fact, the more a woman earns, the less likely she is to have kids.

## Auntie's Day™

Auntie's Day, sponsored by Savvy Auntie®, was launched on July 26, 2009, as an annual national holiday to thank, honor, and celebrate the aunt in a child's life–whether she is an Auntie by Relation (ABR), Auntie by Choice (ABC), or godmother–for all the love and emotional support (and of course fabulous gifts) she offers. For more info, visit AuntiesDay.com.

To draw a line between those with children and those without, excommunicating aunts from the Family Village, isn't constructive and certainly doesn't help the children. That's why instead of labeling women without kids as "childless," I prefer the title "Savvy Auntie." Our lives are not empty without children of our own; rather, our lives are abundant and fruitful with the happiness we are choosing to create for ourselves, including indulging in aunthood. To love, nurture, protect, and help develop a child-not-your-own is a selfless gift that takes time, dedication, and generosity.

I vowed to give aunts as many tools as I could to make their experience as fulfilling as possible. The message of SavvyAuntie.com—and now, of *Savvy Auntie* the book—is that aunthood is a gift. And it's a celebration. It is a celebration so big that it absolutely makes room for the aunties who are not blood related to their nieces and nephews—the aunties who choose to take on that role through friendship, not just family. We even celebrate the random acts of auntie-ing that occur every day.

And as you'll read in this book, that's what we Savvy Aunties are really, really good at: sprinkling a little magic.

# Auntymology: A Few Words About a Few of Our Favorite Words

Now that you're an aunt, you're probably dying to know once and for all the proper way to pronounce the word (as well as its savvier corollary, auntie). Should it sound like the insect that gets in your pants (phonetic spelling 'ant)? Or are you supposed to do that Britspeak thing: *ahnt* (phonetic spelling änt)? Well, just like you and your niece or nephew, it's all relative.

"'Aunt' belongs to a set of words, including 'ask,' 'grass,' 'laugh,' and 'dance,' which are pronounced änt in many accents of British English and 'ant in most accents of American English," explains Jon Herring, a researcher of British accents and dialects for the British Library (and a proud uncle!). "Linguists call this 'the BATH vowel.' Both pronunciations of 'aunt' are equally acceptable, as they are for all BATH words like 'ask' and 'dance,' etc. As a geeky linguist, I have to say that there is not a definitive, correct pronunciation."

The two pronunciations may be equally accepted in academic circles, but among Americans, one is clearly more popular. A study done at the University of Wisconsin found that three-quarters of the U.S. population says 'ant. Of the remaining Americans who prefer änt, most are concentrated along the coast of New England. This particular vowel pronunciation has even been dubbed "the New England broad a," described by Dictionary.com as "having a quality between the [a] of hat and the [ah] of car." Eastern Virginia is another area populated with änt-sayers. Why those two specific regions? Because änt "is most common in the areas that maintained the closest cultural ties with England after the änt pronunciation developed there."

Believe it or not, what we consider to be the American pronunciation of aunt was actually its original pronunciation in England centuries ago—and even today, some British dialects still use the 'ant pronunciation. Herring notes that "it is generally accepted that the 'ant version was the

## *Parlez-Vous Aunté?*

**Ways to say "aunt" around the world . . .**

Albanian: *teze*

Arabic: *khala* (maternal), *ama* (paternal)

Bulgarian: *lelya*

Chinese: *ayi* (maternal), *gugu* (paternal)

Creole: *tante*

Danish: *tante*

Finnish: *täti*

French: *tante*

Gaelic: *aintin*

German: *tante*

Greek: *thea*

Hebrew: *doda*

Hungarian: *néni*

Indonesian: *bibi*

Italian: *zia*

Japanese: *obasan*

Korean: *imo* (maternal), *gohm oh* (paternal)

Polish: *ciotka*

Portugese: *tia*

Russian: *tyotya*

Serbian: *tetka*

Spanish: *tia*

Swedish: *moster* (maternal), *faster* (paternal)

Tagalog: *tita*

Turkish: *teyze* (mother's sister), *yenge* (father's sister)

Vietnamese: *di* (maternal), *cô* (paternal)

Yiddish: *tante*

Yugoslavian: *teta*

original pronunciation, which over time developed into the änt version that you now get in the south of England. Northern speakers will still usually say something similar but not identical to the American 'ant."

I say, use whichever you want . . . or *wahnt.*

I chose to call my website and book Savvy Auntie over Savvy Aunt simply because I'm referred to as "Auntie" by my nephew and nieces. All of my aunts are "Aunties," too. In this book, I chose to stick with the phrase "nieces and nephews"—though I applaud the creative auntie who combines them into niecephews, nephlings, or nephlets—for one simple reason: I would never want to be referred to as one of the auncticles. Or even worse, be dubbed an unclaunt.

# Savvy Auntie Principles

As a proud member of the American Family Village, a Savvy Auntie is entitled to her share of self-evident truths and inalienable rights. Follow these fundamentals for getting the most out of auntiehood (no matter where you live, how involved you are in your nieces' and nephews' lives, or what kind of family you come from).

## Principle #1: Aunthood Is a Gift

Just as a Savvy Auntie is fortunate for each and every niece and nephew who enters her life, the love she shares with these children and their families is an incredibly generous and precious commodity. Although an adoring auntie may feel like she can't help granting her loved ones' every wish and desire, the truth is that everything a Savvy Auntie offers them is a gift. Therefore, a Savvy Auntie knows she is always to be valued and respected in kind.

## Principle #2: The Auntie Is Not the Parent

A Savvy Auntie knows her place in the family and that Mom and Dad's rules and parenting methods come first. No matter what a Savvy Auntie may think they could be doing better, she knows that parenting is not easy and that it's not her place to judge. However, when a parent asks for an auntie's suggestions and thoughts, she is only too happy to help talk things through and find the right answer. (See Principle #9.)

## Principle #3: Rules Are Rules (Even in Your Care)

When an auntie's in charge of the kids, Mom and Dad's rules still apply. A Savvy Auntie discusses rules with the parents beforehand and asks for compromises when they might be too difficult for her to uphold. (Hey, parents have been known to break their own rules from time to time!)

## Principle #4: Priorities Change, Not Love

When a sister or best friend becomes a mom, her ability to always be there for you will probably change. A Savvy Auntie knows that sisterhood and friendship are organic, transforming and growing as life goes on. Just because Mom's schedule is not the same, that doesn't mean her love is any different. No matter how bad the breakup, no matter how exciting the new job, a Savvy Auntie always strives to be flexible in her expectations (as long as she knows she is respected too).

### Principle #5: A Savvy Auntie Never Looks Good in Green

Envy isn't pretty. Whether her younger sister is pregnant (again!) or the children's other auntie is able to see them more often, a Savvy Auntie is confident in all that she is and all that she offers. After all, there's little to be envious about when she has the most amazing nieces and nephews on the planet.

### Principle #6: Respect the Parents, Respect Their Privacy

A Savvy Auntie loves nothing more than gushing about or showing off her most precious nieces and nephews. Most likely, Mom and Dad don't mind at all when the kids' auntie shares photos or stories of the children with close family and colleagues. But before posting pics to more public places like Facebook and Flickr, a Savvy Auntie is sure to ask Mom and Dad how they feel about it first. Likewise, a Savvy Auntie knows that confiding in a close friend about family matters, or even using an anonymous handle to garner feedback from an online forum, is much different from broadcasting a family matter to whomever will listen. A Savvy Auntie is always discreet.

### Principle #7: A Savvy Auntie Manages Expectations (Hers, the Kids', and the Parents')

A Savvy Auntie doesn't promise her nieces and nephews that she'll come over for Christmas and then schedule other plans; that would be mismanaging the kids' expectations. A Savvy Auntie likewise keeps her own expectations in check by acknowledging that she is going to make mistakes and missteps along the way. When she does, she apologizes and remembers that she is not a perfect auntie. To preserve the life she loves outside of her family, a Savvy Auntie sets boundaries as needed to keep her well-being intact and to avoid getting in over her head. For example, does her niece want a bouncy castle at her birthday party? Savvy Auntie may be happy to chip in, but she makes it clear to Mom and Dad that she can't foot the entire bill. A Savvy Auntie never lets her nieces and nephews become her only source of happiness.

### Principle #8: Enjoy Every Minute

A Savvy Auntie knows that children grow up too fast. She takes the time to smell their strawberry-shampoo-scented hair. She never forgets how precious they are.

### Principle #9: Savvy Is As Savvy Does

Knowledge is a Savvy Auntie's best friend. She seeks expert advice (at SavvyAuntie.com!) and is always looking for ways to become better educated about her nieces' and nephews' needs. (Hint: This book is a good start!)

When can you forfeit your Savvy Auntie principles? All bets are off when the parents or legal guardians have made life for a niece or nephew unsafe. If you witness abuse or neglect, it's your duty to investigate, respond, or report it as needed. Safety first.

## How to Use This Guide

This book is meant for the first-time auntie who doesn't know the first thing about babies. This book is for the experienced great-auntie who wants to read up on today's new parenting philosophies and must-get gift ideas for the kids. This book is for a Long-Distance Auntie seeking suggestions for staying involved in her nieces' and nephews' lives. This book is also for the auntie who lives so close by that she's worried about spoiling the kids.

And this book is for every Savvy Auntie—or really, any grown woman—whose life doesn't fit the two-kids-one-husband-two-car-garage mold, and who therefore may need help dealing with those family members, coworkers, and colleagues who don't get it.

One aspect of Savvy Auntiehood I haven't touched on here is auntie-ing the tweenage or teenage niece or nephew. This is for one simple reason: auntie-ing an adolescent mandates a book of its own. There's also not a lot of discussion about nieces and nephews who arrive via adoption or surrogacy, because to a Savvy Auntie, there's nothing different about these remarkable children; therefore, nothing different need be done or said.

My greatest hope is that you'll share this book with every auntie, great-auntie, and godmother you know. Next time your auntourage gets together, bring the book and discuss your thoughts on

## *Auntie Up!* ... What We Love Most About Being an Aunt

Throughout this book, real-life Savvy Aunties will be chiming in with the time-tested wisdom and advice they've gathered from years of personal experience. For starters, here are some of their favorite things about Savvy Auntiehood!

*Being able to act like a big kid!*

—Lisa McConnell, Dallas, TX

*I love the fact that my grown nephews now tell stories to their sons about me. I want to share the same love I had for my nephews with this second generation. My godchildren are also very special to me and let me know that, even though I don't have children of my own, I am loved by so many wonderful and beautiful little ones.*

—Mia Johnson, Rancho Cucamonga, CA

*I love how my nephew's face just lights up when he sees me and he comes running to greet me. I love how he has memorized the way I read books to him and recites the lines back to me with the exact same inflections.*

—Jen Vopat, Elyria, OH

*As the first of four siblings to have kids, I love the role reversal this time around. Now I get to do all of the spoiling with none of the responsibility. It's fantastic!*

—Alyce Barrett, Virginia Beach, VA

*Hugs that bowl you over!*

—Mary Cottingham, Princeton, NJ

*Being able to guide my nieces and nephews in life without the tension that sometimes exists between parent and child.*

—Abbey Kendzior, Chevy Chase, MD

*I love how much more I love my sister now that she is a mommy. It's so different. Her place in my heart grew about fifty times larger just by watching her. She truly is a wonderful mommy.*

—Jessica Alessandrini, Tampa, FL

*Being able to play with them as kids in ways their parents don't have time for.*

—Aileen Markowsky, Mastic Beach, NY

*Nothing feels as great as when they run up and just wrap their arms around you, nuzzle their heads on your shoulder, and give you a kiss—unasked.*

—Karie Warf Price, Houston, TX

*I get to give my nieces and nephews smart-aleck advice and let the parents straighten it out!*

—Wendy Callahan, Silver Spring, MD

a topic. Point out the relevant pages contained herein to a Savvy Auntie who's planning a niece's or nephew's birthday party, contributing to a niece's or nephew's college savings fund, or helping a mom-to-be put together her baby registry. Savvy is always something to be shared.

Including absolutely everything a Savvy Auntie might need to know in this book would be impossible (try as I might!), so I've listed resources in the appendix for any further research you might want to conduct on a specific area of interest.

To pass along your own thoughts, ideas, and experiences to other Savvy Aunties, join in on discussions at SavvyAuntie.com, where you can also read about any updates to the book, and at Facebook.com/SavvyAuntie, which is active with the latest Savvy Auntie news and comments. If you have ideas you'd like to share for future editions, if you've got a question, or if you just want to say hello, you can e-mail me at Book@SavvyAuntie.com or tweet me at Twitter.com/Savvy Auntie. Finally, sign up for the Savvy Auntie Newsletter at savvyauntie.com/l/newsletter.

If you're interested in what's going on with me, I welcome you with open arms at Melanie Notkin.com.

*. . . this book is for every Savvy Auntie—*

*or really, any grown woman—whose life*

*doesn't fit the two-kids-one-husband-*

*two-car-garage mold . . .*

# Welcome to the Auntourage

SO JUST WHO IS A Savvy Auntie–and what is this auntourage she's a part of?

A Savvy Auntie, simply put, is a woman who loves a child who's not her child.

But of course, those little lovebugs are hardly the only thing she's passionate about. A Savvy Auntie's got a life of her own that's packed to the hilt. Perhaps she's getting her graduate degree or about to make partner at her firm. She might be a charitable humanitarian, an actress, an author, or an auntrepreneur. *She's a good friend, a great date, a fantastic spouse.* She's straight or she's gay. And chances are, she's childless–whether by choice or by circumstance–which means she's one of the previously mentioned 50 percent of American women who are not mothers.

The landscape of the contemporary American woman is changing, right along with our traditional notions of family. Today's family is filled with relatives and friends—what I like to call the American Family Village. That's why the typical notion of an aunt—the sister of a parent (a.k.a. Auntie by Relation, as we Savvy Aunties call her; see opposite)—is absolutely not the only kind of aunt in a child's life.

A Savvy Auntie may be an Auntie by Choice (ABC) to her BFF's children. She might be Mom's cousin who lives far away but never misses a birthday. Or she's a passionate godmother to a single mom's baby. Or she's a friendly neighbor who babysits every other Tuesday.

A Savvy Auntie's value is measured neither by relation nor proximity, not by how many presents she gives or by how often she visits, not by her age or by her experience. Her value lies in the joy and positive influence she offers the children in her life, and in the pleasure she takes in living life her own way. She's the modern-day "fairy godmother" who sprinkles a little magic upon the lives of those children she knows—and often, children all around the world.

Of course we know it's not all "magic." A Savvy Auntie is always learning on the job, educating herself just like parents do. This is where her auntourage comes in. It's that circle of girlfriends every Savvy Auntie's got (in real life, or online at SavvyAuntie.com!), there when she needs them no matter what the auntie-related issue—whether it's with the kids, their parents, or her own parents. They are her very own ConfidAunties, ready to lend an ear or a hand when a Savvy Auntie's feeling less than perfect. But you know what, who is? What truly matters is that, by loving and safeguarding her nieces and nephews and all the children in her life the best she knows how, a Savvy Auntie is being the best Savvy Auntie she can be.

So tell us, Savvy Auntie, who are you?

**AUNTIEPEDIA: CONFIDAUNTIE** A Savvy Auntie whose specialty is serving as trust keeper and sounding board to her nieces and nephews, who know they can turn to her with secrets they're not yet ready to share with Mom and Dad. And, of course, everything stays auntre-nous–between niece or nephew and ConfidAuntie.

AS IN:

My nieces and nephews confide in me and turn to me. I think it's the fact that I have a young heart and free spirit that makes them so comfortable with me as their ConfidAuntie. I don't judge or criticize. I just try to help them and, above everything else, let them know that I love them and am proud of them.

–Anita Watson-Cue, Fayetteville, NC

# Auntie Types

## AUNTIE BY RELATION

a.k.a., Classic Auntie. An ABR is the sister or sister-in-law of her niece's or nephew's mom or dad.

*My brother and sister-in-law joke that my parents and I share 50/50 custody of their daughter with them. We have Kate over every weekend and a day or two during the week. We each have the whole setup: complete nursery, gear, clothes, favorite foods. Although I've always wanted children, my niece may very well be the closest I ever come to helping raise a person who shares some of my DNA. I love that she looks like me, and I miss her every day I'm away from her. I feel very vested in making sure she is happy, healthy, smart, savvy, well rounded, and independent.*

—Cortney Gibson, Indianapolis, IN

## AUNTIE BY CHOICE

An ABC is often Mom's or Dad's BFF. Though not technically related to her nieces and nephews, she elects to step into the role of auntie. She's often as close to a niece or nephew as any ABR—and couldn't love them any more if she were.

> *I am an ABC to my best friend's two daughters. They are now nineteen and twenty-three. I taught them how to put on makeup when they were little girls; now the oldest gives me advice on which hair accessories to buy. I taught them to love shopping; now they help me be fashionable. Some of my sweetest memories are of these two young ladies.*
>
> —Terri Claiborne Sasse, Vancouver, WA

## GODMOTHER

a.k.a., Godmommy. A godmother is honored to sponsor a child during baptism. In many cases, godmoms are also ABCs or ABRs. While the role connotes spiritual guardianship, often the godmother is also appointed legal guardian to her godchild should the parents no longer be able to care for him or her.

> *I decided long ago not to have my own children, and felt so lucky when I was asked to be godmother to my best friend's daughter. Although I haven't changed my mind about having kids, I feel pure joy when my little Maya kisses me and tells me she loves me. She was the flower girl in my wedding last year and took the honor so seriously—she was the big hit that day! Having Maya in my life has only made my friendship with her mother that much more special.*
>
> —Danielle Forguignon Azzara, Westfield, NJ

## GREAT-AUNTIE

A generation older than Mom and Dad, a great-auntie often spares no expense in dispensing love and wisdom to all the grandnieces and grandnephews in her life.

*I'm a long-distance great-auntie and travel as often as possible to see my nieces. It is a joyful experience to watch my oldest nephew being a daddy to my two great-nieces—and he's such a good one! I am awed each time I see a glimpse of him in their bright smiles. It is such a gift!*

—Julie Knauff, Dayton, OH

## COUSIN AUNTIE

Sometimes a mom's or dad's cousin is just as close to her or him as a sibling, especially if the mom or dad was an only child. In turn, cousin aunties often feel just as close to a niece or nephew; many are even called Auntie by the child.

*I am an auntie to my cousin's children. I am an only child so this is the best way for me to be an auntie—family is very important.*

—Kimberly Wood, Ballston Spa, NY

## LONG-DISTANCE AUNTIE

The LDA may live far away from her nieces and nephews, but she always keeps them close to her heart. An LDA can also live as close as the next town over but, thanks to her crazy schedule, can't see the kids as often as she'd like. Sometimes an LDA feels more like Guilty Auntie for missing out on baby's firsts and other special occasions. Fortunately, the modern LDA has time-saving, bond-maintaining technology at her fingertips—such as Skype, and for the older kids, texting and Facebook.

*My nephews live in Los Angeles and I live in Kansas City. I never forget to send a card—for birthdays, big accomplishments, and milestones. Even though you can't be there for all of them, a special card (sometimes with a few dollars tucked inside) lets them know they are always on your mind and that they are important to you!*

—Michelle Lynn Fowler, Kansas City, MO

## STEPAUNTIE

Your mom or dad remarries someone with grown kids. Those stepsiblings have kids of their own. Ta-da! Instant auntie. Stepauntie, to be literal. Forever auntie, to be honest.

> *I don't see the word "step." I love and adore all of my nieces and nephews and treat them all with the same love and adoration.*
>
> —Melissa Birchfield, Atlanta, TX

## SINGLE AUNTIE

The Single Auntie may feel perfectly comfortable with her single status, or she may want a spouse or partner someday but hasn't met the right match yet. Single Auntie sometimes feels conflicted between her "single" side and her "auntie" side; likewise, the other adults in her nieces' and nephews' lives sometimes need help understanding and appreciating her lifestyle.

> *I was going away on a singles' vacation and I couldn't wait! The problem was, my sister-in-law was scheduled for a C-section to deliver my second niece or nephew that same weekend. I decided to go away anyway. Hoping to meet someone special on my trip, I told her that I needed to give her kids a future cousin to play with someday soon! My sister-in-law's response? "Go! Have fun! There will be so many family members around that I won't be without support. Go find a great man!"*
>
> —Jamie Koff, New York, NY

## MARRIED AUNTIE

Married Auntie welcomes her spouse into the relationship she already cherishes with her nieces and nephews, offering them extra love and guidance from an uncle (or aunt!).

> *I once heard one of my teenage nephews introduce my husband to one of his friends like this: "This is John; he is just the coolest uncle you could ever have." I was so chuffed, and so was John.*
>
> —Jane Gunnigan, Tipperary, Ireland

## MOMMY AUNTIE

The Mommy Auntie has her own kids and a very special relationship with her nieces and nephews. Women who were aunties first never lose that identity even after they become moms, and while they may not be able to spend as much time with their nieces and nephews as they did before their own offspring arrived, they nonetheless do everything they can to keep the bond just as strong.

*I am the devoted mother of two perfectly respectable children. They have a bedtime, limited TV and computer hours, and are offered fruit when they want a snack. I am also the adoring auntie of two very adorable nieces! The bliss of being an auntie? Doing unto my nieces what I would never, ever do unto my own children! It's like being the sugar plum fairy, Willy Wonka, and Elmo rolled into one.*

—Nancy Rotenier, New York, NY

## PARAUNT

Sounds like, and acts like, a parent. Life brings unexpected surprises and unforeseen circumstances, like when our nieces and nephews come under our legal guardianship. Whether due to unfit parents, illness, incarceration, or untimely death, many aunties are now mommies to their nieces and nephews.

*People always tell me what an "incredible" thing I did by becoming my nephew's mom. There's nothing incredible about it to me. He is my family. He was an innocent kid. I love him regardless of what we call our relationship. I'm the lucky one. I got another son to love.*

—Amie Adams, Springfield, VA

## LESBIAUNT

Since many lesbians don't have children of their own, they may form very close bonds with the children of their friends and families. LesbiAunties enjoy unique opportunities to teach their nieces and nephews about diversity and tolerance. The gay uncle—or "guncle"—is often just as much an "auntie" as any woman!

*When my nieces and nephews found out I was a lesbian, they were much more understanding and accepting than my own siblings had been just one decade ago. We live in a much more tolerant world now, and for many LesbiAunts, myself included, nieces and nephews have almost become our surrogate children. In fact, they kind of think of me as the "cool aunt," just because I'm gay!*

—Jenny Stewart, San Francisco, CA

## TEEN AUNTIE

Becoming an auntie while still in high school or college can change a girl's life. She's realizing she's somewhere between being a child and taking care of one. If it suits her, Teen Auntie may enjoy the financial windfall of being Mom and Dad's go-to babysitter.

*I was about twelve when my first niece and nephew were born. I loved being an aunt at such a young age. They felt like the little brothers and sisters I'd wanted for so long! (I was the youngest of eleven kids, and tried to convince my parents to adopt when I was five.) I would still say that the older set of my twenty-six blood-related nieces and nephews consider me part sister and part aunt. I was a trusted confidante to them. [See: Auntiepedia, ConfidAuntie.] I view all of their accomplishments with immense pride and feel their pain when things go wrong. I definitely think it has made me a wiser and better person to be involved in the upbringing of these fine human beings.*

—Betsy Black, South Orange, NJ

## CHILD AUNTIE

As the modern family changes, sometimes our siblings and stepsiblings are much older than us, making us aunties while still children. Isn't it nice to have a niece or nephew who's like a built-in playmate?

*I have a big family. I am the youngest of seven; the next is ten years older than me, and the oldest is twenty years older, so I grew up a Child Auntie—with some nieces and nephews who are older than me! To an only child or someone from a smaller family, it was strange to see someone older calling me Auntie. It definitely taught me the importance of family. It also taught me that I didn't want to have children of my own while I was still young!*

—Erika Moore, Sacramento, CA

## CHILD-FREE AUNTIE

Some women—single, partnered, married, or gay—have made a clear decision not to have children of their own. However, in no way does this prevent them from becoming fantastic aunties. They may not love kids, but they truly love your kids.

*Instead of a deep desire to be a mom, I had the same desire to be an aunt. It brings me such joy and warms my heart to be an awesome auntie for my niece and soon-to-be-born nephew. I know that being an aunt, not a mom, is what I was made for!*

—Jessica Molloy, Grand Rapids, MI

## SPECIAL-NEEDS AUNTIE

This auntie is special for many reasons. She has a disability, but that never stops her from being a very loving auntie.

*I may have a learning disability, but I am very good at teaching and very creative in my artwork. I hope that someday, my niece and nephew learn that about me.*

—Amy Rosenfeld, New York, NY

## SPECIAL-NEEDS-CHILD AUNTIE

This auntie is blessed to have a special-needs niece or nephew in her life. Because she is often the only other adult trusted by Mom and Dad to understand the child's special needs, she is considered an integral part of the family.

*My special-needs nephew has taught me that being the best is never important; doing your own personal best is. Watching my nephew triumph over things like becoming more articulate or learning to put his pants on himself is so huge for him. I learn from him every day that doing my best is all that matters!*

*—Bridgette Raes, Brooklyn, NY*

## TEACHER OR COACH AUNTIE

The kids in her class or on her team are her children. While she loves shaping their lives and spirits, she regrets having to say "So long" as they move up and on.

*I have always loved kids, but decided at quite an early age that I never wanted my own. I devoted my working years to caring for special-needs children with behavior disorders. That was my life's destiny, to love the children who were deemed unlovable by society, and all too often by their own families. And now, I have the pleasure and privilege of loving my niece and two nephews with all my heart. I can give so much more by having made a conscious decision to not have my own children.*

*—Maryellen Chaplin, Southbridge, MA*

**AUNTIEPEDIA: DEBUTAUNT** A first-time auntie!

AS IN: "Would you like to attend my DebutAunt Ball? It's a party celebrating my initiation into auntiehood. Go to page 202 of this book to find out more!"

## NANNY AUNTIE

A nanny who takes on a large portion of the child-rearing duties when kids are younger may find that those bonds don't go away as they get older. In fact, Nanny Aunties (or Nannties) and their charges often stay in touch for years afterward, marking the special occasions in one another's lives and even maintaining a presence in the lives of the generation to come.

> *I had wanted kids my entire life until becoming a full-time nanny. My gift in this life is working with children, and I've loved every child I've ever encountered. Working with them full-time, though, has opened my eyes to the fact that having my own is not something I desire. Don't get me wrong—I love my nephew and three nieces, like, whoa! But I also love my "me" time. Love to just pick up and go, whether it be traveling or just going to the movies with friends. I have also learned in the last few years that I enjoy sleep; sleep and I have a symbiotic relationship.*
>
> —Janice Plonk, Los Angeles, CA

## FAIRY GODAUNTIE

In the spirit of the "fairy godmother" character commonly found in Disney movies, Fairy GodAuntie is a magical force in a child's life. She appears briefly, for snippets at a time, but always brings joy.

> *I'm three thousand miles away from my nephew, so I'm sure there's a lot of day-to-day aunt stuff I could be doing, especially now that he's four years old and can hold conversations and have fun in the park and the zoo and stuff. But when I do go visit, it's special. I took my cues from my aunt, in remembering how much fun it was when she came to visit me and feeling like I was the only one she was there to see. She was absolutely my Fairy GodAuntie. I get to be the cool aunt with that air of mystery for Evan because I live someplace exotic that he's never seen, and because I never say no to him. That's really the one rule I have for being an aunt: outside of any situation that might put him or anyone else in danger, I never say no to him.*
>
> —Michelle Wiener, New York, NY

## AUNTIE TO THE WORLD

A term coined by one of our favorite Savvy Aunties, writer Elizabeth Gilbert (author of *Eat, Pray, Love* and *Committed*). Auntie to the World gives not only to the individual children she knows; through selflessness, generosity, philanthropy, and charity, she also gives to countless children she's never even met. Although Gilbert minted the term "Auntie to the World" rather recently, benevolent women throughout history have fit the bill. (Think of Mother Teresa and the orphanage she founded in 1955.) Quite simply, Aunties to the World spread their nurturing instincts worldwide.

> *I work as a director of an organization that serves over eight hundred children every day. My whole life is dedicated to other people's children, and that's the way I like it! I don't feel I'm missing out on anything by not having my own. Besides, working with children, I know just how much work they are!*
>
> —Kristin Shaver, Lowell, MA

So that takes care of the auntie part. But what about the savvy?

What all Savvy Aunties have in common is their magical knack for making nieces and nephews feel special. But of course, no two aunties are alike. There are several, if not countless, kinds of savvy . . .

**Savvy Professor Auntie:** a.k.a., SavAuntie. Savvy means smart, and you'll stop at nothing to make sure your niece or nephew is the smartest kid on the block. You're always teaching, whether through educational experiences, brain-bolstering gifts, or ingeniously expounding upon the empirical salience of compiling an elongated vocabulary.

> **FAVE GIFTS:** A high-contrast, black-and-white crib mobile; books; their first computer.

> **FAVE AUNTIVITIES:** Helping with homework; visiting museums; playing word games online.

**Savvy Superstar Auntie:** Always the drama queen, Savvy Superstar Auntie loves all things celebrity, music, fashion, and pop culture.

> **FAVE GIFTS:** A toy microphone; tickets to see the latest tween pop idol; feathered boa.

> **FAVE AUNTIVITIES:** Reading gossip mags before bed; getting together for *American Idol*-themed sleepovers; throwing *iCarly*-themed birthday parties.

**Savvy Eco Auntie:** a.k.a. Auntie Earth, she's focused on making the world a better, cleaner, healthier place to live for her nieces, nephews, and all the people, plants, and animals on the planet.

> **FAVE GIFTS:** Organic cotton jammies; toy trucks made from recycled materials; nature DVDs.

> **FAVE AUNTIVITIES:** Planting a garden; cleaning up local parks; going on nature walks.

**Savvy Sporty Auntie:** No matter what time it is, it's always time to play ball! Or tag! Or hopscotch!

> **FAVE GIFTS:** Their first bike; a swing set; skating lessons.

> **FAVE AUNTIVITIES:** Running a kid-friendly 1K together; coaching their T-ball teams; attending soccer games.

**Savvy Fancy Auntie:** a.k.a. Bon VivAuntie. Everything in life deserves to be done with a touch of class, elegance, and maybe a few extra bucks. Savvy Fancy Aunties know it's the only way to go.

> **FAVE GIFTS:** Your niece's first party shoes; your nephew's first suit; anything glittery.

> **FAVE AUNTIVITIES:** Putting on fashion shows; eating at four-star restaurants; traveling to Paris.

**Savvy Foodie Auntie:** a.k.a. GourmAunt. Feeding her niece or nephew out of a jar just won't do for this foodie. Hand-mixing a medley of brightly colored, organic vegetables is the only obvious choice.

    🎁 FAVE GIFTS: First apron; potted herb garden; kids' cookbooks.

    ✳ FAVE AUNTIVITIES: Watching the Food Network; trips to the farmers' market; taking kid-friendly cooking classes.

**Savvy Domestic Diva Auntie:** You're the hostess with the mostess, excellent at entertaining and renowned for the warm, welcoming home environment you work painstakingly to achieve. Also, you'll be damned if your nieces and nephews don't learn how to arrange Mom's Mother's Day bouquets on their own.

    🎁 FAVE GIFTS: Dollhouse; play tea set; toy vacuum.

    ✳ FAVE AUNTIVITIES: Folding napkins to look like swans; collecting vintage glass bottles; shopping for the perfect throw pillows for her niece's new big-girl bed.

**Savvy Crafty Auntie:** There's nothing you can't make yourself–or for your nieces and nephews–and nothing you enjoy more than passing along your handy habits to them.

    🎁 FAVE GIFTS: Hand-crocheted baby bonnet; baby's-first-year scrapbook; safety scissors.

    ✳ FAVE AUNTIVITIES: Making holiday cards; weaving pot holders; beading necklaces.

**Savvy Traveling Auntie:** The world is your oyster, and you intend to snag every pearl. It's tough not getting to see your nieces and nephews as often, but the experiences you do get to share with them are enriched with tales and trinkets from all your exotic escapades.

    🎁 FAVE GIFTS: A globe; foreign money; one of those T-shirts that reads MY AUNTIE WENT TO . . .

    ✳ FAVE AUNTIVITIES: Naming state capitals; sharing vacation photos; road trip!

**Savvy Giving-Back Auntie:** a.k.a. BenevolAunt. What we get in life is nothing compared to what we give. You are very committed to needy causes, locally and globally, and wish for nothing more than to pass along that do-good spirit to your nieces and nephews.

> 🎁 FAVE GIFTS: **Charitable donations in your nieces' and nephews' names; handmade finger puppets created by artisans in disadvantaged countries; a CD of children's songs that benefits an international nonprofit organization.**

> ✳ FAVE AUNTIVITIES: **Holding charity bake sales; visiting the children's ward of a local hospital; going on a volunteer vacation.**

**Savvy Animal-Loving Auntie:** Animals are this auntie's best friend—next to her nieces and nephews, of course. Not only do you have as many pets as space and your landlord may allow, but you're always looking for opportunities to better the lives of all creatures great and small.

> 🎁 FAVE GIFTS: **A stuffed animal that benefits the local zoo; picture books about animals; a rescue puppy.**

> ✳ FAVE AUNTIVITIES: **Horseback riding; visiting a petting zoo; volunteering at the local animal shelter.**

**Savvy Peaceful Auntie:** a.k.a. BohemiAunt. This chill auntie is all about love, not war. She magically soothes baby with just the lightest touch (and her magical stones). You can hear her say: "Namaste, baby. Namaste."

> 🎁 FAVE GIFTS: **Pacifiers in a slew of pastel colors; a baby Buddha for the nursery; first kiddie yoga lessons.**

> ✳ FAVE AUNTIVITIES: **Quiet meditation; rocking the baby to sleep; picking wildflowers.**

**Savvy Rocker Auntie:** a.k.a. Aunt-Rageous! No need to ask this auntie to turn up the volume. She's got rock 'n' roll in her blood. You can hear her coming from a quarter mile away as she approaches the house on her motorcycle. This bada** auntie has a very soft spot for her baby niece or nephew.

> 🎁 FAVE GIFTS: MY AUNTIE ROCKS **T-shirt; temporary tattoos; rocker booties.**

> ✳ FAVE AUNTIVITIES: **Baby's first music player; visit to Graceland; first open-air rock concert.**

# Celeb Aunties We Love

Stars—they're just like us! The Hollywood obsessed may feel like they're on a first-name basis with these famous females, but to a few lucky kids, they'll always be "Auntie."

**Jennifer Aniston:** Godmom and ABC to BFF Courteney Cox's daughter, Coco, who calls Jen "Nouna"–Greek for "Godmother"! Cox has said that the two like having playdates and even doing yoga together.

**Oprah Winfrey:** An Auntie to the World if ever there was, Oprah often refers to the students at her namesake Leadership Academy for Girls in South Africa as "my dream girls." Oprah is ABR to her nieces Alisha and Chrishaunda, and in the fall of 2010 learned of Aquarius and Andre, her niece and nephew from her long-lost half-sister, Patricia. Auntie O's also an ABC to BFF Gayle King's two kids. She spoke at William King's college graduation, where she quipped, "I'm like his crazy aunt that they let out at commencements."

**Kim and Khloe Kardashian:** The socialites' older sis, Kourtney, welcomed baby Mason in 2009. Both ABRs have gushed in gossip mags and on blogs about what a terrific tyke he is and quipped about which auntie he likes best.

**Ashley Tisdale:** The *High School Musical* star became a DebutAunt at age twenty-five when her older sister, Jennifer, gave birth to niece Mikayla Dawn in 2010. Before Mikayla was even born, Ashley revealed that she planned to be "the spoiling kind of aunt"–which kinda makes her a bit Fairy GodAuntie, too!

**Janet Jackson:** Her relationship with MJ's three children was always a close one, but after the King of Pop's passing in 2009, Janet instantly morphed into a most devoted ParAunt. Numerous news outlets have reported that the kids call her "Mama."

**Kathy Griffin:** The always outspoken comedienne is a Classic/Long-Distance/Single/Child-Free Auntie to her tweenage niece and nephew, two kids she likes to kid with on her reality show, *Kathy Griffin: My Life on the D-List.* On the show's blog, she once wrote, "I don't know how you parents do it, and to be honest, I don't want to know."

**Chelsea Handler:** A fierce Single Auntie but, like many of us, a sometimes-insecure Long-Distance Auntie, Chelsea has written in her bestselling books about all the cross-country flights she's taken to ensure that she would "secure the favorite aunt position" in the eyes of her East Coast niece, Charley, who's also guest-starred on *Chelsea Lately.*

**Jessica Simpson:** She's a one-in-a-million auntie to the world's one-and-only-named Bronx Mowgli. (Mom, of course, is Ashlee Simpson-Wentz.) Jessica's gushed in public about how "over the moon" she felt about becoming a DebutAunt and has called her nephew "a beautiful miracle."

**Ivanka Trump:** Her brother, Donald Trump Jr., is dad to daughter Kai and son Donald III, making auntie another hat stylishly worn by this auntrepreneur/model/wife.

**Kristin Davis:** Although she famously played a married mom on TV, in real life this *Sex and the City* siren couldn't be more different from her on-screen alter ego, Charlotte York Goldenblatt. She once told an Australian newspaper, "I have friends with children and sometimes have moments where I wish I had that. And sometimes it's a good thing I get to go home."

**Tyra Banks:** She's the godmother of Ming Lee Simmons, whose mother, Kimora Lee, is a model-turned-entrepreneur just like Tyra. What fashion sense that little girl's gonna inherit!

**Lisa Ling:** Less than a year after enduring the trauma of her sister Laura's four-month detention in North Korea, journalist Lisa Ling celebrated the joy of becoming a DebutAunt to Laura's daughter–named Li, after her auntie Lisa!

**Kim Cattrall:** The self-described "pretty good auntie" has said she doesn't regret skipping the mommy track and enjoys life as an ABC–just like her groundbreaking *Sex and the City* character, Samantha Jones.

**Renée Zellweger:** An Oscar-winning ABR to her brother's two kids, Renée has pulled no punches in expressing her ambivalence about having kids of her own. "The cool thing about being an aunt is, like, I can leave," she told a London newspaper in 2010. "No offense to my big brother, Drew, but that is slavery. . . . It's a dictatorship. They're little dictators in their crib."

**Beyoncé:** How cool of an ABR is Beyoncé, the torchbearer for "independent women and all the single ladies"? Well, how cool is getting to be your auntie's date to the 2010 Grammys? Uncle Jay-Z even brought then-five-year-old nephew Daniel Julez Knowles onstage with him to accept an award!

**Helen Mirren:** Her turn as Queen Elizabeth II may have won her an Oscar, but Savvy Auntie (to nephew Simon) is another role she was born to play! In 1997, she told a British newspaper, "The aunt/nephew relationship is a fab one, almost as good as being a grandmother. Simon is exactly like my son, except that he's not. There is no chastising, only spoiling, and you can be racy, and break all the rules. I've never wanted kids but I'm very happy to enjoy other people's, and I'm incredibly lucky to have Simon."

**Rachel Zoe:** The celeb stylist knows that being an awesome auntie never goes out of style. She celebrated nephew Luke's bar mitzvah first by tweeting the proud news–then by taking him to the NFL Pro Bowl! Her niece, of course, enjoys endless shopping sprees with Auntie Rachel.

**Kylie Minogue:** A proud ABR to sister Dannii's kids. As a treat for her nephew, Daniel, Kylie appeared with the Wiggles on their DVD *The Wiggles Go Bananas*.

**Queen Latifah:** Costarring with Paula Patton in the 2010 rom-com *Just Wright* led to the Queen becoming an ABC to Paula's firstborn. She even hosted Paula's baby shower!

**Rachael Ray:** Besides publishing recipes on her website for foodstuffs like Aunt Angie's Lasagna and Aunt Clara's Taco Casserole, this media mogul knows how to stand up to tough questions about her choice to go child-free. She once told an interviewer, "I have an enormous amount of hours that have to be dedicated to work. For me personally, I would need more time to feel like I'd be a good mom to my own child. I feel like a borderline good mom to my dog." When questioned whether she felt she was missing out on something, she replied, "I don't feel like I am. I really don't."

**Julia Roberts:** The year after she became a "pretty woman," she became a SABR (Single Auntie by Relation) to Emma Roberts. Now married with three kids of her own, Julia's a devoted Mommy Auntie who's credited with helping Emma get her Hollywood career off the ground.

**Cameron Diaz:** Three nieces and a nephew are lucky to call Cameron "Auntie," who told a reporter in 2010, "My family is the most important thing to me. My family and my friends–that's my greatest wealth." While she describes herself as a "pretty good aunt," kids of her own aren't a necessity. "I'm not opposed to it happening. Having children changes your life drastically, and I really love my life. Children aren't the only things that bring you gratification and happiness, and it's easier to give life than to give love. So I don't know. That kind of change would have to be either very well thought, or a total mistake–a real oops!"

# Fauntasy Aunts

Aunties run rampant throughout great works of fiction—be they books, movies, or TV shows. A few of our faves:

**Aunt Augusta,** the eccentric adventuress created by author Graham Greene in his 1969 classic novel *Travels with My Aunt.*

**Aunt Bea,** Ramona Quimby's aunt in the Ramona Quimby books and the *Ramona and Beezus* movie.

**Aunt Bee,** the affable Auntique on *The Andy Griffith Show.*

**Aunt Clara,** Samantha's charming, bumbling ABR on *Bewitched.*

**Edna Garrett,** part Teacher Auntie, part Nanny Auntie, part ABC, part ParAunt for the girls of 1980s TV who were learning the "facts of life."

**Auntie Em,** Dorothy's ParAunt in *The Wizard of Oz.*

**Aunt Esther,** sister to Sanford's late wife on *Sanford and Son,* whose catchphrase–usually invoked by her intense distaste for Sanford–was "Watch it, sucka."

**Aunt Jackie,** arguably the most fascinating character on *Roseanne;* she went from self-esteem-lacking Single Auntie to (still single) Mommy Auntie to well-intentioned Married Auntie, back to Single Auntie (albeit one with newfound confidence), and finally, in the series finale, a LesbiAunt!

**Auntie Mame,** the fabulously bohemian title character of the bestselling 1955 novel that spawned a play and movie of the same name–and of course, the 1966 smash Broadway musical *Mame.*

**Mary Poppins,** the world's most beloved Nanny Auntie, star of the many books, classic movie, and Broadway musical that bear her name.

**Aunt May,** Peter Parker's ParAunt in the *Spider-Man* movies and comics.

**Monica Geller-Bing,** ABR to brother Ross's two kids: Ben, the one he had with his lesbian ex-wife, and Emma, the one he had (by accident!) with ex-girlfriend Rachel on *Friends.*

**Aunt Norris and Lady Bertram,** protagonist Fanny Price's well-to-do ABRs, who hold widely different views on the importance of love, security, and money, in Jane Austen's *Mansfield Park.*

**Patty and Selma Bouvier,** Marge Simpson's older twin sisters, making them ABRs to Bart, Lisa, and Maggie Simpson on (can you guess?) *The Simpsons.* Patty is the show's sole LesbiAunt.

**Aunt Viv,** Will Smith's whip-smart ParAunt on *The Fresh Prince of Bel-Air.*

**Aunts Zelda and Hilda,** the co-dwelling ABRs on *Sabrina, the Teenage Witch.*

# What Our Savvy Auntcestors Have to Say

Where would we—the entire planet, that is—be without these selfless, tireless women? Some of the most important, iconic aunties to the world were real-life ABRs; others were ABCs; all of them were driven to make the world a better place, one person at a time. And based on some of their best bons mots, we're pretty sure they would've liked being called Savvy Aunties, too.

**Florence Nightingale** (1820-1910), NURSE DURING THE CRIMEAN WAR: "The real fathers and mothers of the human race are not the fathers and mothers of the flesh. For every one of my 18,000 children, I have expended more motherly feeling and action in a week than my mother has expended on me in 37 years."

**Mother Teresa** (1910-1997), CATHOLIC NUN, HUMANITARIAN: "Do not think that love, in order to be genuine, has to be extraordinary. What we need is to love without getting tired."

**Helen Keller** (1880-1968), SEEING- AND HEARING-IMPAIRED ACTIVIST: "It is not possible for civilization to flow backwards while there is youth in the world. Youth may be headstrong, but it will advance its allotted length."

**Anne Sullivan** (1866-1936), HELEN KELLER'S TEACHER: "Children require guidance and sympathy far more than instruction."

**Emily Dickinson** (1830-1886), POET: "My friends are my estate."

Jane Austen (1775-1817), NOVELIST: "I have been a selfish being all my life, in practice, though not in principle."

Shirley Chisholm (1924-2005), CONGRESSWOMAN: "The emotional, sexual and psychological stereotyping of females begins when the doctor says: 'It's a girl.'"

Margaret Mead (1901-1978), ANTHROPOLOGIST: "I must admit that I personally measure success in terms of the contributions an individual makes to her or his fellow human beings."

Grandma Moses (1860-1961), PAINTER: "I look back on my life like a good day's work, it is done and I am satisfied with it."

Rosa Parks (1913-2005), CIVIL RIGHTS ACTIVIST: "Memories of our lives, of our works and our deeds will continue in others."

Amelia Earhart (1897-1939), AVIATOR: "I want to do it because I want to do it."

Joan of Arc (1412-1431), FRENCH MARTYR AND CATHOLIC SAINT: "One life is all we have and we live it as we believe in living it."

# Auntiescopes: What's Your Sign, Auntie?

Still not sure what type of auntie you are? Look to the stars! Jeannine Mercurio, a counseling astrologer and SavvyAuntie.com's resident soothsayer, tells all about the auntstrology that makes you unique!

###  Aries: Jumping-out-of-Airplanes Auntie

You are the warrior auntie, not waiting for a cab, a Cobb salad, or a rainy day to spend that bonus. You drive the nephews to the zoo, watch them feed the goats, then hit up a sample sale—all on the same Saturday afternoon. You squeeze in fun and somehow, because you've got some sort of pact with Father Time—life is short! have fun now!—you get it all done. You love to take charge; you are not into being closely supervised, so you rise to the top instead. Call your own shots, Auntie Aries!

###  Taurus: Patient Auntie

Taurus types take time to create. You are the planner, the steady one, and will surely prove to be a consistent and comforting figure in the lives of your nieces and nephews. When the kids come over for movie night, you are ready with home-baked cookies. You are the auntie most likely to make baby's first quilt.

###  Gemini: Multitasking Auntie

You're e-mailing three friends and planning your BFF's baby shower while being interviewed over the phone by a prospective employer for your dream job. Time? Ain't got none. Inner peace? You're still searching for it. You give your neighbor's youngest daughter a pep talk before her school-play audition while buying toothpaste at the pharmacy. You eat breakfast at 6:00 P.M. Thank God for coffee.

###  Cancer: Nurturing Auntie

You are calm, a maternal leader. You are kind, resourceful, and excellent at managing crazy. You keep your plants alive and your relationships healthy. When you bake brownies for your three teen nieces, you not only know that the girls will go wild for the cute, stiletto-shoe shapes you cut their treats into, you also remember to mix up three distinct bowls of batter—one with nuts, one without nuts, and one that accepts some traces of nuts. You solve everyone's problems.

##  Leo: Royalty Auntie

You perch yourself in the front row at the kids' soccer games and dance recitals, donning a fitted leopard blazer from Betsey Johnson. Every coach, referee, and single dad wants to know if you're single. Even your nieces and nephews can tell what a head turner you are, which means they love going anywhere with you—and since you're so naturally theatrical, where they often go with you is to see the latest Broadway show. Your mantra is: Dress up every day and bring on the glamour.

## Virgo: Practically Perfect Auntie

When you babysit in winter, you bring homemade vanilla soup and warm cashmere socks. By the time Mom and Dad return home for the night, not only will the kids have brushed their teeth, but you'll have packed organic, gluten-free sandwiches for their lunch boxes tomorrow. You've done the research on health, your chakras, and the global economy. You are the practical, detail-obsessed auntie who knows a million little things about a million and one different topics.

## Libra: Peacekeeping Auntie

You are an excellent mediator in all relationships; you never let the nieces and nephews fight. You put out the fires and teach love, harmony, and (why not?) a little rock 'n' roll. A master at using your words, you balance out wild cards and turn chaos into serenity.

## Scorpio: Go-to Auntie

Power is your middle name, Auntie, which is why you're the one others turn to when they need direction—at work, within the family, or while driving the car. You turn junk into gold and you never lose your groove. You're who others want to see leading the charge.

## Sagittarius: Gypsy Auntie

You are the see-it-all, do-it-all, teach-it-all auntie, traveling to new worlds and designing your own destiny, one destination at a time. You turn out for every party, but you're never fashionably late since you've got a plane to catch right after; you've been just dying to see the Mayan ruins.

###  Capricorn: Self-Made Auntie

Not only did you blaze your own career path, you've also planted your own garden to enjoy once the workday's done. You celebrate your latest promotion by having the triplets over to your place for the weekend, ordering in gourmet pizza and helping them build a fort in your gorgeous, recently renovated apartment. You let them make a mess and track dirt on the floor—it's all OK, because you know you're living your dream.

###  Aquarius: Outside-the-Box Auntie

You are ahead of your time and you make your own blueprint for life. You are an original. You work for yourself, invent new jobs, or change gigs every couple of years. The children in your life see you as a revolutionary.

###  Pisces: I'm OK, You're OK Auntie

You are one empathic, intuitive auntie. The kids come to you when they need to be held, consoled, or inspired. You make them squash their fears and blaze new paths for themselves. You are always encouraging them to try new things—whether that's eating a tomato, auditioning for the school band, or attempting a cartwheel.

# The Aunticipation!

## 3

THERE'S NOTHING LIKE THAT SO-AMAZING moment when you first find out that you're going to become an auntie. There's also *so much to learn!* You're not alone if you feel that way. The truth is, the majority of first-time moms and dads likewise have little clue beforehand about what the next nine months have in store for them. They'll probably read up a storm of pregnancy guidebooks to catch up—information I've distilled down to the essentials here in this chapter.

Remember, the mom-to-be is going to need all the support she can get when it comes to stocking up on baby stuff, dealing with pregnancy's less-than-pleasant side effects, figuring out how she'd like to give birth, deciding on a name. (And Auntie, I know that you might need some support during this time as well. Another woman's pregnancy—even when it's the person you're closest to in the world—can bring up all sorts of feelings, including ones you didn't even know you had. We'll talk; see the Auntre-Nous section.)

So, how on earth is all this going to get done in nine months? With Auntie's assistance, of course!

# What to Expect When She's Expecting

We've all heard of trimesters and morning sickness. Other pregnancy details we're a little fuzzy on. But by savvying up on what to expect, you'll be better prepared to ask the right questions, say the right things, and be the best support you can be. The following pregnancy timeline, courtesy of NYC-based ob-gyn Dr. Miriam Greene, will get you up to speed. By the way, Dr. Greene also played an ob-gyn on TV. She delivered Miranda's baby, Brady, on *Sex and the City*!

Here's another little bit of trivia. Did you know that pregnancy lasts about ten lunar months, counting from the first day of a woman's last menstrual period? So by this confusing measure, she's already two-ish weeks pregnant by the time of actual conception. There—you're savvier already.

## First trimester: 1–12 weeks

### WEEK 5
An embryo is developing. Mom's missed her period by now.

### WEEK 6
A little beating heart!

### WEEK 7
Starts experiencing morning sickness. At this point, she may get an initial early scan, which will confirm her due date and may inform her if she's having multiples.

### WEEK 8
Mom's body starts changing. She might lose her waistline and her boobs may swell a bit.

### WEEK 11

Embryo's now called a fetus. Placenta is working on its own now, providing nourishment.

### WEEK 12

Morning sickness has peaked and will begin to subside. Now or in the next two weeks, Mom will undergo a noninvasive sonogram, a.k.a. nuchal translucency, for chromosomal disorders (such as Down syndrome), which is recommended for all moms-to-be, no matter their age. The doctor also looks at the nasal bone of the fetus and runs a blood test.

## Second trimester: 13–27 weeks

### WEEK 13

This is usually when Mom and Dad start sharing the news as the risk of miscarriage diminishes significantly.

### WEEK 15

If Mom's a skinny chick, she'll start to show.

### WEEK 16

Is Mom feeling a mite gassy? Surprise—it's the fetus moving! Although it's so tiny, she won't feel any specific body parts (legs, feet, hands, etc.). A blood test performed this week will check for spina bifida; it'll also be compared to Week 12's test to further diagnose any chromosomal abnormalities. An amniocentesis may also be performed, where a needle is inserted into the amniotic sac to retrieve a small amount of fluid. Despite rumors to the contrary, a large majority of women report feeling no discomfort during the procedure (a local anesthetic is used) and the risk of serious complications such as miscarriage are way less than 1 percent.

### WEEK 17

Mom's probably put on five pounds. Thwart body-image issues by telling her how absolutely radiant she looks with child. (See: Mompliments.)

### WEEK 18

First ultrasound is done if not done earlier; parents may find out fetus's gender. (If the parents don't tell you, don't ask. That's why God created greens and yellows.)

### WEEK 19

By now at latest, a radiologist should perform a 3-D scan of Mom's belly, producing a photograph of the fetus. You can see if it looks like Mommy or Daddy (or Auntie!).

### WEEK 20

Halfway there! Mom's belly pops out because the uterus is growing along with the fetus inside. Mom should feel energetic and healthy, with tons of energy.

### WEEK 21

Weight gain may be up to ten pounds. Offer to help out with errands and keep the mompliments coming! This is a great time to check out some fab maternity clothes together. It's also when she goes for a final scan to observe the fetus's brain. It might not be her last scan, but it's her last "official" scan.

### WEEK 23

Mom's just cruising along, happy as a clam. Start to check out baby furniture with her.

### WEEK 25

Crazy pregnancy dreams may ensue. Very hormonally driven and vivid, they will of course concern a pregnant woman's anxiety about labor and motherhood.

## You Glow, Girl!

Yes, pregnant women really do "glow"! "You see it," Dr. Greene says. "When you're pregnant, more estrogen is circulating through your body, and this causes the production of more oil and the retention of more fluid in your face. So your face fills out, lines are gone, and you glow from the oil!"

### WEEK 26

The ob-gyn will schedule a glucose screening test between now and Week 29 to check for gestational diabetes, a pregnancy-related blood sugar condition that affects about 5 percent of expectant women (and is a higher risk for women carrying twins or multiples). Starting around this time, some mothers-to-be might experience Braxton Hicks contractions (a.k.a. false labor), and these might continue to term.

### WEEK 27

Many women say the second trimester is their favorite part of pregnancy—and by now, the party's ending. Uterus begins to press on Mom's diaphragm, causing mild discomfort.

## Third trimester: 28–42 weeks

### WEEK 28

Mom starts seeing her health-care provider every other week. Weight gain is up to 17–24 pounds. As if that's not bad enough, she's probably got leg cramps, hemorrhoids, swelling, and itchy skin—oh, and for the next four weeks, hormones will really affect her mood, so tread lightly. Since the fetus can now recognize Mom's voice from the womb, hope that Mom keeps hormonally driven cursing about cramps, swelling, and so on to a minimum. This is also when she takes her glucose challenge test.

### WEEK 30

All major organs except the lungs are almost fully developed in the fetus. Mom starts to have trouble finding a comfortable sleeping position, so may be extra tired.

### WEEK 32

Fetus is about four pounds. Mom may be experiencing constipation and heartburn. May begin to take childbirth classes at this time.

### WEEK 33

Weight gain starts to slow down for Mom while the fetus will gain about four to six ounces a week from now until birth.

### WEEK 35

Fetus around five and a half pounds. Cervix starts to soften and thin out.

## WEEK 36

Weekly doctor visits begin. Mom's doctor will be taking a vaginal test to be sure there's no beta strep bacteria in the vaginal canal. Fetus will be in a head-down position inside the womb.

## WEEK 37

The baby starts to move down into the pelvis in preparation for delivery. That's when the doctor says the fetus has dropped, and Mom literally begins to breathe easier. This is a good week to help pack Mom's overnight bag for imminent hospital stay. She may start to have fears and concerns about labor, so make yourself available to talk as best you can.

At the due date, 97 percent of all fetuses are headfirst (also known as "vertex"). The other 3 percent are either breech (booty is first) or transverse (baby is sideways). In those cases, if the fetus cannot be moved to a vertex or head-down position manually, a C-section will most likely ensue.

## WEEK 39

The baby's head is now pressing up against Mom's bladder; she makes frequent trips to the ladies' room. (If you're taking her to her last movie before birth, get her an aisle seat!) Baby may be just over seven pounds.

## WEEKS 40-41

Mom's due date has arrived! But for most first-time mothers, the baby won't arrive precisely on time. She may have to wait until Week 41. Oh, the aunticipation!

Once Mom's water breaks, she must go into labor. If it's not happening naturally, the baby must be induced. Induction is done with an intravenous drip with a synthetic form of oxytocin called Pitocin.

# Mompliments: Say This, Not That

Following is what moms and moms-to-be told me they most—and least—want to hear when they're pregnant.

MOST: "You're barely showing!"
LEAST: "How much weight have you gained?"

MOST: "You can't tell from the back."
LEAST: "By how your butt looks, I'm guessing it's a girl."

MOST: "You're glowing!" (Some moms cautioned that they never believe this one; see "You Glow, Girl!" on page 46.)
LEAST: "How often do you have to go pee?"

MOST: "You look radiant!"
LEAST: "The extra weight looks good on you."

MOST: "Congratulations!" (And then smile!)
LEAST: "How long did it take you to get pregnant? Was it planned? What fertility drugs did you use? How many tries did it take?"

MOST: "I hope I look as good as you do when I'm pregnant!"
LEAST: "I guess you're 'eating for two.' Go ahead and chow down."

MOST: "Wow, you're six months pregnant?! I didn't even notice."
LEAST: "Is it twins? You're looking so big!"

When in doubt, admiring her maternity wear is always a wise choice. Touching her belly without asking is NEVER a good idea.

# Auntre-Nous: Straight Talk for the Childless Auntie

Any Savvy Auntie knows what a special moment it is when you find out you're about to become an auntie (especially when it's for the first time), and you're probably elated to hear that a sibling, cousin, sister-in-law, or close friend is expecting. You might even be an inner-circle, BFF auntie-to-be, privileged as one of the first to know the big secret, sometimes even before Dad does. That's amazing, right? Maybe even the most amazing news you've ever heard? It absolutely is.

But what if that awesome news comes with a but: But what about me? What if you are . . .

❋ the older sister who always thought she'd have a baby first?

❋ a twin who sees her sibling "moving ahead" without her?

❋ past the age by which you always assumed you'd have kids of your own?

❋ trying unsuccessfully to conceive, or dealing with a recent miscarriage?

❋ enduring the endless paperwork needed to carry out an adoption or surrogacy, with no finish line in sight?

❋ a single woman who sees her married friend reaching yet another milestone without her?

❋ married to a man with children from his first marriage who is "done" having kids?

❋ at the peak of a career you love and don't want to take a break to have a baby, even though you believe you've only got a few "good" pregnancy years left?

Whatever feelings you have about the situation, they're valid. These days, the modern woman without kids is besieged by all sorts of mounting pressures, internal and external. While you may be trying to sort out your own emotions—Is this jealousy or something else? Do I really want kids of my own right now, or ever?—everyone else seems to be counting your remaining eggs on your behalf, telling you to "hurry up" and have a baby. Many folks, including veritable strangers, even do you the favor of listing your options for you:

- ✼ **You could have a baby on your own, sans significant other.**

- ✼ **Have you thought about freezing your eggs?**

- ✼ **Just adopt!**

- ✼ **Why don't you trick your boyfriend (or hey, even a one-night stand) into getting you pregnant?**

- ✼ **You could always try in vitro!**

- ✼ **Go meet a man, fast! Get online, go to bars, meet my husband's coworker's brother's best friend from college!**

It's never ending. And that's the problem.

The good news about today, of course, is that child-free lifestyles are becoming more and more accepted, and for those of us who do worry about having kids later on in life, we've got medical advances that really do up a woman's chances of conceiving a healthy child. (See Chapter 10 for lots of helpful info on the subject.) The downside is that we also live in a world where celebrities' "baby bumps" are considered headline-worthy, where couples go online to solicit IVF-treatment donations—in other words, a world where information that used to be intimate and private, like the state of your ovaries and whether or not you choose to make use of them, is now considered public domain. People (who barely know you, no less) have got no problem telling you, "Oh, you should do what my cousin did. She had her twins at forty-five through IVF. You have plenty of time!"

To make matters worse, it often seems that only childless women in committed or legally binding relationships are justified in airing their fertility-related distress. Picture this: A married woman in her early forties expresses to a group of friends how frustrating her infertility issues have been for her and her husband. They sympathize accordingly. Then her single, thirty-nine-year-old friend chimes in with, "I, too, have been pretty sad lately, mourning that my delayed success in forging a lifetime romantic partnership may be impeding my future chances of creating the family I've long dreamed of having!" Aaaand . . . awkward silence.

The single woman in that scenario is really mourning two separate things: not finding a suitable partner during prime childbearing years, and not having what she's long dreamed and hoped for.

# How to Handle Your Grief

WRITE IT DOWN.

"Journaling often leads to greater acceptance and personal understanding," says Stephanie Baffone, a board-certified mental health therapist who focuses on grief and infertility. "It helps to process anger, stops that anger from being misdirected, and allows you to exhale the toxicity of your loss."

FIND A COMMUNITY.

It is profoundly healing when someone else says, "I know how you feel." And in the age of new media, it's easy to find others with similar life experiences. (Psst! How about on SavvyAuntie.com?)

GIVE YOURSELF AN END DATE.

Yes, you need to take time to feel your grief. As Baffone says, "If you don't grieve, grieving will do you." But put a deadline on it, after which you'll do your best to reembrace all that's positive in your life and move forward.

DON'T TELL THE MOM-TO-BE.

Even if you two are close, try not to share any negative feelings with her. Little good can come from confronting her when emotions are running high within both of you. However, if you really feel you need to later on, you can "calmly acknowledge that, in the face of her happiness, you are feeling a sense of personal loss," Baffone says. "Tell her how she can be helpful to you in return. No one's sense of loss or happiness trumps the other's."

TAKE DELIGHT IN THE CHILDREN AROUND YOU.

You might think that what you need right now is a break from the kids in your life, but really, you should capitalize on your role of auntie. Being an auntie comes with perks exclusive just to you–that's what this book celebrates, after all!

Now, before you decide to just give up and go join a convent (probably the only place where a woman's childlessness doesn't come under questioning), let's talk about your situation using some more positive jargon. Instead of fretting over "fertility issues," what if you embraced "the biology of belief"?

This is the thinking of Dr. Christiane Northrup, bestselling author of *Women's Bodies, Women's Wisdom: Creating Physical and Emotional Health and Healing.* As one of the country's leading authorities on women's health, she knows firsthand what the main culprit of fertility anxiety is: fertility treatments.

"Because we now have reproductive technology—which is wonderful when needed—but just because we have it, now women are hearing that after the age of thirty-five, their chances [of conceiving] are less and less," Northrup says. "No one was telling women this before fertility treatments came along."

And in reality, the facts about fertility actually skew very much in your favor, Auntie:

❋ **According to the 2002 Survey of National Growth, only 1 in 8 couples struggles with infertility.**

❋ **The Reproductive Science Center of New England states that men are responsible for 40 percent of all fertility problems among U.S. couples. (Women make up another 40 percent; 20 percent are due to incompatibility issues or reasons unknown.)**

❋ **Numerous studies have shown that a very low percentage (3 to 5 percent) of women experiencing infertility problems need to resort to in vitro fertilization (IVF) to conceive a child.**

❋ **The chances that a fertility problem is successfully treated through conventional therapies, says the RSC, is 85 to 90 percent.**

Just remember that getting pregnant isn't something that your sister or friend did to you, and the fact that she managed to get pregnant doesn't mean you never will. No matter what, a new life is always, always something to celebrate. Which we will commence doing—starting right now!

# Let's Party, Baby!

There's no better cause for celebration than a new life coming into the world. So naturally, upon hearing that a niece or nephew is on the way, a Savvy Auntie is going to want to throw a big ol' baby shower.

Showers once meant awkward small talk and tiny sandwiches, but luckily times are changing. From backyard BBQs to wedding-scale blowouts, today's baby shower is a whole new to-do. Also gone are many of the old-fashioned, fuddy-duddy rules and etiquette surrounding showers as new customs and conventions become the norm.

The bad news is that, if you're a DebutAunt who's never been to a baby shower, or a great-auntie who hasn't attended one in ages, you might be feeling pretty out of your party-planning element.

So to get you started, I consulted with Carley Roney, editor in chief of TheBump.com, on the basic who, what, where, when, why, and how of showers.

## WHO *hosts a baby shower, especially if more than one of us wants to?*

The hostess is usually a close friend, sister, or sister-in-law of the guest of honor. Parents or in-laws traditionally do not host—but again, many people nowadays could give a hoot about traditions, so don't be surprised if a mother or mother-in-law wants in.

Luckily, cohosted showers have always been popular, so if several people are eyeing the hostess title, why not join forces? One of you may have the best living room or backyard, another is a fabulous cupcake baker, and a third loves nothing more than spreadsheeting a guest list. It's also a way to cut down on individual costs, and maybe even get to know some of the mom-to-be's friends and family a bit better.

Another common custom is to throw more than one shower. It's perfectly normal for a woman to be thrown a shower by her family, another that's just close friends, and so on. If the mom-to-be lives far away from family, she may even hop on a plane to attend one of her showers. So if the cohosting idea doesn't work out, then you, as a Savvy Auntie, will simply do a fab job on your own throwing the mom-to-be one of many showers. (Yours will be the best one, natch, but no need to brag. OK, you can brag a little.)

## WHAT *happens at a baby shower, exactly?*

If you've ever been to a wedding shower, it's like that, except usually with games and/or a theme. Guests arrive, everybody eats, the guest of honor opens her gifts, you play a few games, everybody goes home. You're done!

Now, you can take that template and twist it any way you like; the rules are less rigid than they used to be. Shower themes and games may not be completely passé, for example, but they're certainly not required. While some Savvy Aunties and modern-day moms might find them tacky or annoying, preferring a more sophisticated or low-key gathering, other friends and family may be disappointed if you don't go with a theme or offer games to play. Don't worry—there are countless, cool ideas out there (and in here!) for themes and games that will ensure a grand time for all.

## WHERE *should I hold the shower?*

At your place if there's room enough. At another Savvy Auntie's house if she's got more space. In a restaurant that's ideal for private luncheons or parties, if you want something a bit swankier. At the spa or the bowling alley, if that's what Mom wants!

Alternatively, throwing it at Mom's place isn't off limits, and it does eliminate having to transport a bunch of bulky baby items back to her place afterward. However, someone has to clean the house before guests arrive and pick up all that gift wrap after they leave. Even if you hire a housekeeper or recruit a team of Savvy Aunties to help clean, "having company over" might still stress Mom out. This day should be easy and hassle-free for her, so you be the judge of whether the commotion would stir up too much emotion.

## WHEN *during a woman's pregnancy is the right time to throw her a shower?*

Although baby showers used to take place much sooner, these days they're typically held around the seventh month of pregnancy. At the least, many moms like to have it after they've revealed the baby's gender, if that's something they've chosen to share, so they can round out their baby registry accordingly and you can tailor your shower look and theme as needed.

Throwing the shower after the baby's born can also be the right decision for a number of reasons: if a pregnancy has been difficult; if the parents-to-be want to first make sure their adoption or surrogacy goes through successfully; if the shower is also the best opportunity for friends and family to meet the baby for the first time; or if a mother's cultural background dictates that a shower before birth is bad luck.

## WHY *are showers women-only?*

Our thoughts exactly! While "just us ladies" may still be the norm, coed showers have been growing in popularity. It's shocking, but some women believe that coed showers might even be (gasp!) more fun than single-sex ones, and they're certainly more memorable.

The mom-to-be may have a lot of gay friends who are tickled pink about becoming guncles, so why exclude them? Or Mom and Dad, if they're the first of their social circles to become parents, may both have a lot of single friends; what Single Auntie wouldn't want to get her flirt on with a guy who's secure enough in his manhood to purchase and gift-wrap a baby-bottle warmer? Also, Dad will use all this gifted baby equipment almost as much as Mom, so shouldn't he be there to open presents and thank people in person?

Having said that, you can't call it a coed shower and then break out the pastel invites and cucumber sandwiches. You'll have to de-frill things: serve beer, go for a hard-rock sound track, and so on.

## HOW *many people should I invite?*

If the mom-to-be belongs to a close-knit auntourage, you may want to keep it to those select few. If she's got tons of Aunties by Relation (ABRs), Aunties by Choice (ABCs), and great-aunties,

# Auntique vs. Savvy Auntie Showers

Want to host a bash with contemporary flash? Here's the lowdown on what's in (a.k.a., right up a Savvy Auntie's alley) and what's out (leave it for the Auntiques!), courtesy of TheBump.com's Carley Roney.

| AUNTIQUE | SAVVY AUNTIE |
|---|---|
| Showers that last all afternoon | An early-afternoon, two-hour shower |
| A sit-down lunch | Appetizers only, or an early brunch |
| Anything with the crusts cut off | A "cravings" buffet of the mom-to-be's fave foods |
| Pink and blue pastels | Cool color combos like blue/brown and periwinkle/cream |
| A nursery-rhyme theme | A *Wizard of Oz* theme (Nicole Richie and Joel Madden did it!) |
| Playing the "Poopy Diaper" game (Don't know what that is? Lucky you.) | Playing poker! (The buy-in? A pack of diapers!) |
| Guessing the baby's due date | Baby-shower Bingo |
| Candles for favors | Edible favors (How 'bout a cupcake and a cute milk carton?) |

you may wind up with a list of fifty people. Most important, of course, is who the mom wants in attendance, so build the guest list together. Second most important? Making sure there aren't so many guests that Mom couldn't possibly open all their presents before the party's over. Everybody—everybody—wants to see their gift opened! Third most important: your budget has to work with the size of the party. Whether or not you tell the mom-to-be how much moolah you're planning to spend, hopefully she'll know not to get too crazy. Obviously, if the shower's going to be a casual cookout, then you can afford a larger guest list than, say, tea at The Plaza.

# *Auntie Up:* What's a Great Gift for Newborns?

**The first gift you give a newborn niece or nephew can be so special—and therefore, very intimidating to choose! I asked Savvy Aunties about the real-life presents they've bestowed upon their nieces and nephews to fabulous fanfare. Bonus: What's most memorable is often less expensive!**

*My favorite children's book with a handwritten inscription from me. I gave my niece and nephew their own copies of* Where the Sidewalk Ends. *It was my favorite when I was a kid, and I hope to be able to share it, and my love of reading, with both of them.*

—Jessica Molloy, Grand Rapids, MI

*I hand-knit booties, caps, and thumbless mittens, or a soft teddy bear with a hand-knit blanket. [Just remember, Auntie, no stuffed animals in a newborn's crib, and no blankets either unless they're very lightweight and breathable.]*

—Pauline Parker Brannigan, New Milford, CT

*I've made scrapbooks prior to baby's arrival. I decorate the pages but leave blank spots where Mom and Dad can just insert the baby pictures. Seeing as it's a crazy time for new parents, I've received many compliments on this gift. It's sort of become my trademark, and I enjoy giving something from the heart.*

—Mireille Roy, Sudbury, ON

*I cross-stitched birth announcements with the name, date of birth, and weight for each of my nieces and had them framed.*

—Paula Malozowski, Bethesda, MD

*Since my nephew lives two hours away, I made a Build-a-Bear for him with a "recordable heart." I recorded a message telling him I love him. I also gave him the book* On the Night You Were Born *and taped inside it a picture of the two of us on his birthday with a little note.*

—Shannon Lahiff, Toledo, OH

*A silver cup with the child's name on it.*

—Patricia Rossi, Tampa Bay, FL

*I think it's good to give a niece or nephew something that is popular or relates to the year of birth. I have a niece who was born in 1996, and I live in Atlanta, so I got her a keepsake from the 1996 Summer Olympics, which were held in Atlanta!*

—Denise Lobodinski, Marietta, GA

### The Baby Sprinkle: Celebrating the Second (Third, or Fourth) Time Around

One of the most pressing questions about baby showers is, Are showers for Baby #2 tacky? The answer: not as long as it's done tastefully. Enter the baby sprinkle!

Held in honor of an expecting mom who already has children, a baby sprinkle is a scaled-down version of a shower. That means smaller guest list, smaller budget, and, because Mom already owns big-ticket baby items like a crib and a car seat, smaller, more inexpensive gifts, like onesies and diapers. (The exception is when a new baby comes quickly on the heels of the last one, in which case a second crib, car seat, and so on is needed. Ditto if Mom has twins the second time around.)

Depending on the ages that Mom's other kids are and whether or not her friends also have kids, a sprinkle may more closely resemble a children's playdate. Then again, a sprinkle might be her excuse for a rare, adults-only afternoon, in which case a "No Pampers Just Pampering!" party would be perfect. (Hire someone to give the guests manis and pedis!)

Throwing a baby sprinkle is ideal for the Savvy Auntie who didn't get to participate in the previous baby shower. For example, a Married Auntie who wasn't yet a part of the family when a sister-in-law's first shower took place may love the idea of throwing her a sprinkle.

# Brand-Name Baby Booty

Newborn necessities have changed lots since we were newborn nieces ourselves. In fact, there are enough must-have products and lusted-after labels on today's baby-goods market to make a shopaholic auntie swelter—and to make a Savvy Auntie feel totally unsavvy and out of her element.

So think of this section as your baby-gear GPS, pointing you toward what baby needs and what brands to know. To give you the hippest list possible, I've enlisted Lyss Stern, founder of New York City's Divalysscious Moms social network.

### Prams

Prams, a.k.a. carriages, are designed for the baby to lie flat and are only recommended for newborns up to twelve weeks old. Traditional pram brands often boast elegant design and beautiful craftsmanship (and can cost thousands of dollars).

The poshest prams are:

* **Silver Cross Balmoral**

* **Inglesina Classica Pram**

* **Stokke Xplory**

* **Bugaboo Cameleon**

* **Mutsy 4Rider**

## Strollers

Strollers—which keep kids in a reclined or upright position and are suitable through toddler-hood—have become ridiculously tricked-out vehicles that often come with accessories and add-ons. There are several kinds: jogging strollers, all-terrain strollers, bike strollers, travel strollers, double (and more!) strollers. (The simple, pop-out kind that you likely rode in as a wee one? That's called an umbrella stroller.)

On-the-go strollers for moms-a-go-go:

* **Bumbleride Flite**

* **Quinny Buzz**

* **iCandy Cherry**

* **Baby Jogger City Mini**

* **Maclaren Volo**

* **Mamas & Papas Urbo and Sola**

* **Taga**

## Getting (Too?) Attached

There are countless cool attachments available for all of today's stylin' strollers–from scooters that allow for big-sib ride-alongs, to parasols, fans, cup holders, even iPod docks and speakers! If you're planning on buying a stroller for the parents, leave something in the budget for attachments (often sold separately) or choose one that comes with attachments you know Mom and Dad would die for.

# Safety Savvy

I understand that big-ticket baby items can be a large budget consideration. But since safety comes first, if you are considering buying a used stroller, crib, and so on, or even an older model on clearance, check out its safety record and recall information first. You can find safety info on lots of child products at www.cpsc.gov/cpscpub/prerel/category/child.html.

Also, bear in mind that baby gear has undergone some big design changes over the years in the name of safety. For example, in late 2010 the sale and manufacture of drop-side rail cribs were banned; since 2000 more than thirty infant deaths have been attributed to them. Infant car seats face backward now instead of forward, and all child restraints now carry an "expiration date" to prevent use after a product has become obsolete.

## Cribs

Sleeping options abound for tiny newborns (see Newbornzzz . . . ). But once your niece or nephew can sit upright, the tall, slatted sides of a crib are a safety necessity. Many cribs on today's market can convert into toddler beds, a plus for cost-conscious parents and aunties.

Classy cribs for so-now nurseries include:

* Stokke Sleep

* The Luxo Crib by Bloom

* Argington Bam Collection Bassinet/Crib Set

* Bratt Decor Venetian Crib

* Corsican Furniture Company Pumpkin Crib

## High Chairs

Cutesy, ruffled, straight-backed high chairs are out; curvaceous, minimalist, multifunctional feeding chairs (as they're now often called) are in. Bonus: The newfangled, European-designed feeding chairs often provide years more use.

Go find these fashionable feeding chairs!

❋ **Bloom Fresco Loft**

❋ **Phil&Teds Highpod**

❋ **Mamas & Papas Go Eat and Loop**

❋ **Astro High Chairs by Valco Baby**

❋ **Stokke Tripp Trapp**

❋ **Calla High Chairs**

# Newbornzzz . . .

For the first four to six months, a newborn's got a lot of sleeping options. Mom and Dad may choose any of the following baby bunks for your niece or nephew:

A *bassinet* is a basketlike bed, often used during the first three or four months of infancy. Because it's small and portable (thanks to wheels or handles), Mom can easily keep your niece or nephew close throughout the day and especially for nighttime feedings. Many parents also like using something tinier than a crib because of the cocoonlike sleeping environment it provides.

A *cradle* can likewise be used for the first few months. Depending on the model, a cradle usually isn't as mobile as a bassinet; however, many cradles boast beautiful design and craftsmanship that will look just precious in a nursery.

A *cosleeper* is a contraption used when practicing attachment parenting (see page 106). It allows an infant to sleep in the same bed as Mom and Dad, or attached to the side of their bed.

## Babe, Bed, and Beyond

Baby linens and accessories are often too cute to resist, but remember that, for safety reasons, pillows, duvets, top sheets, and stuffed animals cannot be kept in a crib with a sleeping niece or nephew. A properly outfitted crib needs only a waterproof mattress protector and, on top of that, a fitted sheet.

There are also crib bumpers, padded panels intended to keep a baby from hurting himself or herself against the sides of a crib; however, some safety advocates believe these pose a suffocation hazard, creating a greater threat than they solve. If your niece's or nephew's parents want to use bumpers, shop for "breathable" ones and make sure they're properly and securely installed.

For the same reasons, any blanket you give your newborn niece or nephew should be lightweight and breathable. Wearable blankets, a.k.a. sleep sacks, are a new trend in safe sleeping accessories.

Crib skirts, like bed skirts, are another decorative option for dressing up baby's new bed. As these don't come into contact with a sleeping baby, they are perfectly safe to use.

If you really want to buy some sort of toy for the crib, what your newborn niece or nephew will most appreciate (as much as a newborn baby can appreciate something) is a mobile to look up at. Black-and-white ones are popular because babies aren't able to distinguish colors until they're about three months old.

# Daddy Diaper Bags!

**Is your brother about to become the most dapper daddy ever? Diaper Dude is a line of guy-friendly diaper bags, many designed to look like messenger bags and backpacks, that even the poshest pop will prize.**

## Diaper Bags

When designers like Gucci and Burberry get into the diaper-bag biz, you know that this must-have accessory has officially reached chic status!

Mom may want to don one of these designer diaper bags:

❋ **Petunia Pickle Bottom**

❋ **Not Rational**

❋ **StorkSak**

❋ **Skip*Hop**

❋ **Timi and Leslie**

❋ **Fleurville**

## Baby Bottles

These days, most parents opt for bisphenol A–free plastic bottles or old-fashioned glass bottles. (A chemical found in many plastics, BPA can leach into breast milk or formula fluid when a bottle is heated up.)

Boss BPA-free bottle brands would be:

❋ **BornFree**

❋ **Tommee Tippee**

❋ **Dr. Brown's Natural Flow Classic bottles**

## Pacifiers

The American Association of Pediatrics recommends using pacifiers to lower the risk of SIDS (Sudden Infant Death Syndrome). Some moms worry that pacifiers may interfere with breast feeding, but most opt to use one in exchange for, well, a pacified baby. BPA-free pacifiers, like baby bottles, are what's popular.

Popular passies to purchase are:

- **Mams**
- **BornFree**
- **Tommee Tippee**
- **Elodie Details**
- **PersonalizedPacifiers.com and MyPacifier.com**

## Swings

Baby swings have become even more souped-up than strollers, available with countless different swinging speeds, seat angles, side supports, sound tracks, sensations, and vibrations. A swing designed for newborns may specifically mimic Mama's womb, while one for older babies might provide the same ergonomic cradle and comfort as a pair of adult arms.

As far as specific brands go, just go classic. Beloved Graco and Fisher-Price still offer the best swings on the market.

## Playards

Nowadays, what we used to call playpens go by playards or "pack and plays"—because Graco's Pack 'n Play line has pretty much cornered the playard market. Many playards come with gear that allows them to also function as bassinets and changing tables. All playards are easily foldable for storage. If you're worried about one clashing with your decor, try playard slipcovers like Coverplay, which come in lots of cute designs and can be thrown into the laundry.

# The Layette

Generally, newborns come home to a layette, a set of clothes and other soft items they need from day one. Stores usually carry preselected layette sets for boys, girls, or yet unknown, or you can create your own with the items you like most. While a Savvy Auntie naturally wants the layette she selects to be the cutest of them all, remember that Mom and Dad are also looking for practicality—and may not get much use out of one deemed "too special" for daily use.

Here's a practical layette list:

* Short-sleeve, long-sleeve, and/or kimono-style onesies (7-10)

* Wearable blankets (a.k.a. one-piece nightgowns) or footed cotton PJs (2-3)

* Leggings and tops that can be easily taken off and on (2-3)

* Socks (they don't need shoes until they start walking) (6-8)

* Machine-washable receiving and swaddling blankets (2-5)

* Burp cloths and/or cloth diapers (10)

* Hooded towels for bath time (2)

* Bibs (2-3)

* Sweater (1)

* Bunting or snowsuit (weather depending, of course) (1)

* Hats (cotton or fleece, depending on the climate) (2-3)

* Scratch mitts so baby doesn't scratch her cute little face before she gets her first newborn "manicure" (1-2)

How many of each will really depend on how often the laundry will be done.

## Don't Forget the Accessories!

Stock up on these sundries so that Mom, Dad, Auntie, and baby can keep clean, stay healthy, look cute, and/or stress less!

* ❋ **Baby bottle warmer**

* ❋ **Baby cream**

* ❋ **Baby hairbrush**

* ❋ **Baby monitor**

* ❋ **Baby nail clippers**

* ❋ **Baby-safe sunscreen**

* ❋ **Baby thermometer**

* ❋ **Baby wash**

* ❋ **Baby wipes**

* ❋ **Diapers for newborns**

* ❋ **Diaper cream/rash ointment**

* ❋ **Diaper pail**

* ❋ **First aid kit**

* ❋ **Hand wipes**

* ❋ **Massage cream or oil**

* ❋ **Night light**

* ❋ **Nontoxic cleaners**

* ❋ **Rinsing cups (for bath time)**

* ❋ **Smoke and carbon monoxide alarms**

* ❋ **Sink tub (a tub that fits into a kitchen sink)**

* ❋ **Washcloths**

# Extreme Makeover: Nursery Edition

Hoping for decor that's a little more cosmopolitan than cutesy-poo, your newborn niece's or nephew's parents have turned to you, natch, for some savvy design advice. I asked Stacie Krajchir-Tom, a Los Angeles–based author, lifestyle expert, and creative consultant (who's decorated her nephews' rooms to immense goos and gahs) for some cool ideas.

## Eschew Blue (Pink, Too)

Well, maybe not entirely, but what about trying a "grown-up" hue like chocolate brown as the main wall color, paired with an accent of powder blue or baby pink? Yellow and gray are wonderful for boys and girls alike, as is a turquoise-and-orange combo.

## Collection Perfection

When Stacie's nephew Cole was born, the family called him "Birdie," so Stacie started collecting beautiful bird figurines made out of glass, ceramic, and paper to display in his room. Cole loved Auntie's aviary so much, he named each and every bird!

## Circle Around

Paint circle-shaped canvases (available from any art supply store) in hues that tie into the room's palette, or paint designs or stripes on them. (Use masking tape to help keep your lines straight.) The circles make fun accents and can be moved around and painted over as the room transforms into an older child's bedroom.

## Remember Mementos

Hang on to "first" items, like the first paintbrush your niece or nephew uses, and display them in shadow boxes with a little note and the date. Visitors will go gaga for these keepsakes, and when your nieces and nephews are all grown up, they'll always remember Auntie as their creative mentor.

## I, Uh, Door You!

Have every family member sign the nursery door using colorful pens or markers. Even better, sketch a family tree on the door first, then let everyone sign their corresponding branches. (A Long-Distance Auntie can be specially denoted with a doodle of an airplane next to or encircling her name.)

## You Gotta Hand It to 'Em!

Designate one corner of the room for a family handprint collage. (Think how much the older sibs will love dipping their little digits in paint and putting them on the wall without getting in trouble for it!) As baby gets older, he or she will delight in showing off this unique art installation to visitors.

# Ten Essential Nursery Books

No newborn's bedroom is complete without its own little library! These titles are recommended by Karen Gallagher, founder of the Lollipop Book Club:

*Goodnight, Moon* by Margaret Wise Brown, illustrated by Clement Hurd

*Peek-a Who?* by Nina Laden

*Pat the Bunny* by Dorothy Kunhardt

*Where Is Baby's Belly Button?* by Karen Katz

*Dear Zoo* by Rod Campbell

*Guess How Much I Love You* by Sam McBratney, illustrated by Anita Jeram

*Dinosaur Roar!* by Paul and Henrietta Stickland

*Brown Bear, Brown Bear, What Do You See?* by Bill Martin Jr., illustrated by Eric Carle

*Jamberry* by Bruce Degen

*The Napping House* by Audrey Wood, illustrated by Don Wood

# Niece- or Nephew-Proofing Your Home

A Savvy Auntie can't wait to start hosting her baby niece or nephew with (and sometimes without!) his or her parents for Sunday gatherings, special occasions, and even extended stays. But she would never do so without first prepping her pad every way possible to make visits convenient, comfortable, and safe.

(Most of these to-dos, Auntie, needn't really be done until your niece or nephew is big enough to sit and crawl. But I recommend taking care of it all now. It's an easy way to score points with the parents. Think how supersavvy you'll look!)

Here's how to safeguard your home, courtesy of Dr. Leigh Vinocur, a board-certified ER physician:

�֍ Get down on your hands and knees to figure out, from a child's point of view, what types of dangerous hazards a young niece or nephew can get into.

✖ Stairs are a big cause of injury for very young kids. Prevent access to them with removable gates, which are simple to install when your niece or nephew is over, and easy to fold flat and store when not.

✖ Safety latches on cabinets and drawers (available at any hardware store) will keep all potentially poisonous household cleaning chemicals out of reach. (If your cabinets have close-set knobs, looping a rubber band tightly around them will also keep doors from opening.) Never store any sort of chemical substance in old food containers so kids don't mistake them for something edible.

✖ The most common cause of child poisoning, however, isn't household chemicals; it's prescription medications. Colored pills can look like candy to small kids, and seeing Auntie "eating" them will make them think they're OK to try. Never refer to your prescription meds as "candy" in front of the nieces and nephews, no matter how good they make you feel!

✖ Store all meds (Rx and OTC) out of reach of little hands, in safety-latched drawers and cabinets.

✖ Keep house plants, plastic bags, and dangling cords (as you might find on venetian blinds) out of reach, as they pose poisoning, suffocation, and strangulation hazards.

# The Organized Auntie on . . .
## Making Room for a Niece or a Nephew

Turn your posh pad into an accommodating auntie abode! Swap in a few furnishings that can stow niece and nephew necessities without compromising your carefully curated decor. Here are recommendations from Janice Simon, CPO, our resident Organized Auntie:

KEY PIECE: **Storage ottoman or bench**

SPACE-SAVING SAVVY: **Does double duty as a coffee table or footstool.**

SHOPPING TIP: **If it opens on hinges, make sure it's got safety latches to keep small fingers safe.**

KEY PIECE: **Under-the-bed bags or boxes**

SPACE-SAVING SAVVY: **Hides under the bed!**

SHOPPING TIP: **Look for ones with handles to make them easy to retrieve.**

KEY PIECE: **Decorative, lidded boxes**

SPACE-SAVING SAVVY: **Great for tucking away small items, like books or toys.**

SHOPPING TIP: **Get some that match your decor and will look good stashed on a shelf or stacked in a corner.**

KEY PIECE: **Magazine file boxes**

SPACE-SAVING SAVVY: **Another great place for kids' books.**

SHOPPING TIP: **Wood and metal file boxes are handsome but pricey. You can opt for supercheap cardboard ones, then decoupage with wrapping paper, fashion mag pages, and so on.**

KEY PIECE: **Vintage suitcases–stack 'em to whip up a multifunctional end table!**

SPACE-SAVING SAVVY: **Great for blankets, burp towels, toys, art supplies, stuffed animals, etc.**

SHOPPING TIP: **Best for shabby-chic or otherwise vintage environs.**

KEY PIECE: **Over-the-door shoe organizer**

SPACE-SAVING SAVVY: **Revolutionizes diaper-changing duties! Stash powder, pins, individual nappies, and so on.**

SHOPPING TIP: **Shoe organizers with clear, plastic pouches let you see everything at once.**

* Cover your outlets with plug covers. Sharp furniture edges can also be covered.

* If you live in a high-rise, make sure there are guards on the windows.

* If your interior doors have locking mechanisms, tape over them when nieces and nephews are over so they can't accidentally lock themselves in a room.

* When cooking, always use your stove top's back burners and turn pot handles in toward the middle of the stove.

* Heat-packing aunties should always keep guns unloaded, locked, and far away from kids. In fact, your nieces and nephews shouldn't even know that you have them.

# Birthing Methods

Most women give birth in a hospital with an obstetrician present and an epidural on hand. However, some moms-to-be have alternative birth plans. In fact, there are so many ways to customize a baby-birthing experience that it can be hard to keep them all straight.

For example, "natural childbirth" is a term often used to describe any vaginal birth, regardless of where, with whom, or on what drugs it occurs. But more and more, the term refers strictly to a vaginal birth that forgoes drugs or other medical assistance.

What's most important to a Savvy Auntie is not which method Mom wants to use, but what you should know and how you can help. Check out our recommended roles for you on the big delivery day, Auntie!

## Vaginal Birth

The most common and *traditional type of delivery,* usually done in a hospital with the help of physicians, nurses, and equipment monitoring Mom's and baby's health during labor.

### SAVVY AUNTIE'S ROLE

Unless Mom insists on having you in the labor room, stay clear. If labor is long, though, ask if she'd like some company, especially if she doesn't have a spouse or partner with her. A shared walk around the maternity ward during early labor is an example of a little something Mom might really appreciate. She'll also need ice chips (the closest thing to food that most doctors allow women in labor to have), someone to help her review any delivery procedures (like breathing exercises), and a few reassuring words to keep her calm.

## Cesarean Birth, a.k.a. C-section

Mom's obstetrician may plan a C-section in advance if he or she determines that, *for the mother's or baby's health,* it's best to forgo a vaginal birth. (Reasons can include anything from a contracted pelvis to fetal distress to a too-big baby.) An unplanned C-section may occur if complications arise during labor, such as an umbilical cord wrapped around the baby's neck. Either way, a

C-section is major surgery. A four- to six-inch incision will be made just above her bikini line and the baby (or babies) will be taken out via her abdomen and uterus.

### SAVVY AUNTIE'S ROLE

It's one thing to have surgery. It's another to have surgery and a newborn who needs feeding and coddling and a bunch of well-meaning visitors waiting to see you—all while your hormones are totally out of whack. Having a Savvy Auntie on hand can prove a lifesaver. The new mom may be in pain and have trouble walking, so even helping her to the bathroom can be much-appreciated assistance.

## Lamaze

Developed by French obstetrician Dr. Fernand Lamaze in 1951, the Lamaze technique is based on the practice of psychoprophylaxis, which roughly translates from medspeak into "the mind prevents." (It shares the same root as prophylactic, which is pretty ironic when you think about it.) *Focused on a woman's breathing during labor and delivery.* Lamaze is designed to help her better understand what's happening to her physiologically and to better manage her pain during childbirth. A common misconception about Lamaze is that it advocates against using drugs during delivery, but in truth, if Mom wants an epidural or any other medically administered pain relief, that's entirely her choice. Lamaze classes usually run six to eight weeks in the time leading up to the due date.

### SAVVY AUNTIE'S ROLE

About 41 percent of women who give birth nowadays are single, and although some may have a mate, others will need (and love!) having a Savvy Auntie for a Lamaze partner. If you are offered the job, make sure that you can attend all the classes with her and that you will be in town around her due date. If you are unable to commit, as much as you want to say yes, you must tell Mom so that she can find the steady partner that Lamaze requires.

## The Bradley Method

Inspired by the numerous animal births he witnessed growing up on a farm, Dr. Robert A. Bradley's namesake method advocates *drug- and surgery-free delivery* as the best means of achieving healthy childbirth. Every properly accredited Bradley course lasts twelve weeks, includes a

130-page student workbook, and focuses on healthful practices such as proper nutrition, pain-reducing labor techniques, relaxation, and breathing. Also known as husband-coached childbirth (the title of Dr. Bradley's 1965 book on the subject), the Bradley method places a strong emphasis on Dad's (or any coach's) presence during delivery.

### SAVVY AUNTIE'S ROLE

Help Mom study! And if there's no dad or partner, a Savvy Auntie may be asked to step into the role of coach.

## Water Birthing

As women seek a more relaxing labor experience, water births have grown in popularity. *A warm bath helps Mom focus on the birth and not the pain,* say water-birthing advocates. Because the water replicates the aqueous environment inside Mom's womb, delivery is also much less shocking for the baby. The baby receives oxygen from the umbilical cord until it's cut, so he or she won't breathe while underwater. (No need to worry about an accidental drowning, Auntie.) Many hospitals and birthing centers have birthing tubs, but some parents choose to rent a birthing tub for an at-home delivery. (A plain, old bathtub doesn't have the needed legroom; almost always, birthing tubs are designed to include the mom, the caregiver, and the dad.)

### SAVVY AUNTIE'S ROLE

If there is no dad, Mom may ask you to be there with her—if not in the tub, then in the room.

## Acupuncture/Acupressure

Some moms-to-be may choose to have acupuncture and/or acupressure during different stages of pregnancy and even through labor and delivery. Advocates claim that using these *traditional Chinese medicines can reposition a breech baby in the womb more effectively* than the Western practice of external cephalic version (ECV), manually moving the baby by pushing on the mother's abdomen. Acupuncture has also been used to induce labor and to manage pain during delivery.

### SAVVY AUNTIE'S ROLE

Whether or not you believe in alternative birth methods, be supportive. Mom needs support, not distractions.

## Hypnobirthing

Women who practice hypnobirthing use certain *breathing techniques during labor to focus themselves on the birth itself, not the fears surrounding it.* The belief is that labor pains are accelerated by fears, and if Mom can alleviate those, delivery will be a natural, calm experience.

### SAVVY AUNTIE'S ROLE

If Mom needs a little help getting started with her hypnobirthing exercises during labor, make sure you know how to get her focused. (Rehearse beforehand!) If she seems to be in a lot of pain during labor, it's not your job to encourage her to take drugs she doesn't want to take. It will just stress her out even more.

## Other Delivery-Day Definitions

### DOULA

Basically, *a doula makes sure that Mom's birthing experience happens to her liking.* She (doulas are virtually always a she) helps the mom-to-be develop her birth plan during pregnancy. She's also present throughout labor and delivery, providing emotional support and expediting communication between the patient, her health-care providers, and family members. Postpartum, her job is to ease Mom's transition into motherhood through education, information, some physical assistance, and more emotional support. (DONA International, which certifies doulas, denotes a difference between birthing doulas and postpartum doulas, although individuals often get certified in both.) Doulas can be privately hired by a parent, and some work as hospital employees or volunteers. Some studies have shown that working with a doula can reduce labor complications and anxiety as well as the need for painkillers.

### MIDWIFE

Usually but not always a nurse, *a midwife often conducts at-home births,* although she can be on call at a hospital as well. Unlike a doula, a midwife is a pregnant woman's primary medical caregiver before, during, and after birth. She is certified to carry out prenatal checkups and actually deliver the baby—unless complications arise, in which case an ob-gyn is brought in or the patient is taken to a hospital. States' laws differ as to what certifications a midwife needs, whether her services can be covered by insurance or Medicaid, and whether she may perform her duties outside of a hospital.

### EPIDURAL

The most popular form of medical pain relief during labor, an epidural anesthesia is administered via an injection into a woman's spinal canal and a catheter. Some parents and health-care providers worry that an epidural can have negative side effects on the baby, but there has not been much research conducted on the subject to either support or refute that conclusively.

### EPISIOTOMY

The procedure involves enlarging of a woman's birthing canal by making a surgical incision along her perineum. It's performed under a local anesthetic and sutured up after birth. Episiotomies have been on the decline in the United States for decades, as research has shown they're no "better" than the vaginal tears that may occur naturally during childbirth.

# Delivery-Day Dos and Don'ts

* **DON'T expect to be in the delivery room. That is VIP access only, and unless you have been Mom's birthing partner during all her prenatal classes, you are not on the list as her plus-one.**

* **DO develop an "Auntie Plan." About a week before the due date, discuss what the mom-to-be would like your responsibilities to be for the big day. It may involve your staying at the hospital to keep long-distance relatives informed of any updates. If she's got other kids, you may be most needed back on the home front to pick them up from school, babysit, and so on.**

* **DO dash back home if labor lasts awhile to whip up some homemade food for the rest of the brood stuck back at the hospital. You'll start earning Savvy Auntie brownie points before your niece or nephew even gets here! (In fact, come to think of it, you should definitely bake brownies.)**

* **DO whatever laundry and housework needs doing back at the parents' house. Feed and walk the pets; make sure things are tidied up nicely; put a lovely final touch on the nursery with a vase of fresh-cut flowers. (Tulips are a savvy pick because they're a low-fragrance flower; strong scents may make a newborn baby fuss. Make sure the buds haven't opened yet so they'll be in beautiful bloom by the time Mom and baby arrive home.) Return to the hospital with a pillow or blanket that will add a touch of home to Mom's hospital stay.**

❋ DON'T forget your cell phone! You'll need it to alert Mom's list of friends and family she wants notified. (Get their names and numbers before the big day arrives.) If you've got a smartphone, use it to coordinate Mom's network of friends via e-mail or Facebook.

❋ DON'T overstay your welcome once the little boo finally arrives. Mom is probably dying for some sleep, and if it's the parents' firstborn, they're going to want some quality time alone with baby and each other.

# Baby Naming

When we hear we're going to be an auntie, one of the first things we want to know is what the baby's name will be. Will the baby be named after a loved one? Will the name be trendy? And of course, most important—will Savvy Auntie approve?

The celebrity baby boom of the past few years has opened the floodgates as far as what's fair game in a name: comic book characters, ingredients for fruit salad, countries, musical instruments, and so on. It's also led to a minibacklash as old-fashioned names like Sophia, James, Elizabeth, Noah, and Grace enjoy a comeback. Add on to all this name craziness the fact that most of us have been imagining names for our own hypothetical children since we were children ourselves, and naming a niece or nephew can go from family-bonding joy to total buzzkill.

In other words, Auntie, etiquette is necessary when taking on the testy topic of baby names.

Laura Wattenberg, author of *The Baby Name Wizard: A Magical Method for Finding the Perfect Name for Your Baby,* offers some advice for the name-enamored auntie.

### What role can I play during the naming process?

If your relative or close friend chooses to share naming choices with you as a sounding board, offer to be discreet. With all the things that end up being passed around during prebabyhood days—ultrasound pictures, morning-sickness tweets, dates of scheduled C-sections—a sacred, secret name-share may be just the thing that bonds Auntie and Mommy.

### I'm hoping that the baby will be named for a beloved family member. How can I egg this idea along?

You can cast your vote if asked, but beware: modern parents are less likely to choose a name they don't think is stylish. If that's the case, suggest that Great-Uncle Gary be honored with a middle name or even an initial.

### How can I up my chances that the name I suggest will be picked?

The problem is, we all want a name no one else is using, but we also want a name everybody likes. That's a hard combination to find! However, here's a trendy tip: soft-sounding vowels (Olivia, Emily) are in, harsh consonants (sorry again, Uncle Gary) are out.

### What if I want to call my niece or nephew by a nickname?

Your own, unique nickname for a niece or a nephew is a charming way to cement the auntie-child relationship, make your niece or nephew feel special, and begin sharing other just-the-two-of-you traditions and activities down the road. But before you drop an unexpected "Izzy" or "Joshie" within earshot of other family members, ask Mom and Dad first. With so much thought going into name selection, parents these days are very protective of names and may not want nicknames. Today's naming trends are about elegance and creativity, whereas nicknames are often considered too friendly and informal—not what parents are going for. That means no Alex for Alexander, Nick for Nicolas, or Gaby for Gabriella.

If the parents don't easily agree to the idea of a nickname, try suggesting one that isn't the ordinary or obvious choice. There are very unusual nicknames that date back centuries. Back in the 1880s, when practically every fourth girl was named Elizabeth (a name that's been making a comeback lately), Betty, Beth, Eliza, and Lise were all employed as nicknames. A Nicolas can also be a Cole, Colin, Niels, or Niko. Mary can become Mamie, May, or Mare.

Of course, sometimes the best nicknames come to you spontaneously, so if you can't find the right one at first, take your time. When it does come to you, your little Niki or Lili will love his or her new nickname!

## What's the fascination with celebrity names?

The truth about celebrity names is that they set trends only when we're ready for them. We generally like the sound of a name we hear often, like Mylie. So as a result, we begin to hear similar-sounding names like Marlie and Kylie. And if people don't like the way a name sounds? Sorry, Madonna—your fame may be global, but your moniker has yet to hit a trend list.

## What if I hate the name?

When you first hear the proposed name of a niece or nephew, make sure whether this is the parents telling you the name or asking your opinion on it. Hearing the name is not an automatic invitation to share your opinion. If you say you don't like the name, you'll probably hurt their feelings. And that's not savvy.

But I understand that a name can say a lot. It sends a message, and that's why we care so much. For example, one of the most sensitive issues surrounding a name is, to put it delicately, trailer trashiness. But you probably don't want to tell Mom and Dad that. Instead, find facts on which you can build your argument. Facts are better than emotions in this situation. Google the proposed name; does the website for an adult entertainer pop up? Remind Mom that her daughter will likewise be googling her name as soon as she's tall enough to reach a keyboard. You might also show how a name is losing popularity, which has the effect of aging the person who goes by it. Why should little Richard endure a name that makes him sound like he's already a grown-up—or worse, saddles him with the nickname "Little Richard"?

Be sensitive, and remember that once the name is given, there is no choice but to say, "How lovely!" After all, you will love this child regardless of his or her name. In the end, it probably doesn't matter as much as you think it does right now.

*But I wanted that name!*

Let's say one of the names Mom and Dad are contemplating is one that's been on your baby name list forever. It's an icky feeling, and understandably, you probably want to yell something very babylike, like, "I called it!" or "No stealing!"

Unfortunately, there's no such thing as "dibs" on a name. It's a first-come, first-serve operation. So if you really, really have your heart set on a name, have that talk with the parents before they begin to share their selections, especially if it's the name of a beloved family member or if it carries on a family tradition.

Alternatively, it's really not the end of the world to have two children of the same name in a family or among best friends. How about using distinct nicknames to differentiate between the kids when the time comes? It just might be the spark that starts a new family tradition, or that sets two babies on the path to BFFs.

*. . . a sacred, secret name-share may be just the thing that bonds Auntie and Mommy.*

# Congrauntulations!
## You're an Auntie!

4

THE MOMENT YOU'VE BEEN WAITING for is finally here. *You're about to meet your niece or nephew for the first time!* The only thing that could possibly spoil your excitement is that you've never actually held a newborn before, so you're a little worried that you might get it wrong. You've heard that infants can't hold their heads up on their own. Speaking of heads, aren't theirs really soft and dentable? And what if the baby wiggles out of my arms? What if the baby hates being in my arms and starts to scream? What if I panic? WHAT IF I DROP THE BABY?! OMG I'M GOING TO DROP THE BABY!!!

Calm down, Auntie. You won't drop the baby. (That includes when you're feeding, changing, or

## Size Matters

Premature newborns weigh up to about five and a half pounds at birth (but may lose a little weight in the first few days after) and can fit into the palm of your hand (although I don't recommend that you hold them with just one hand until you get the hang of things). Newborns carried to term weigh about seven and a half pounds, on average, although they can weigh anywhere from five and a half to ten pounds, and measure about twenty inches long (more or less depending on their weight). Babies gain about three times their birth weight in their first year and grow about one and a half times in length. So hang on to every little moment, Auntie. They literally grow so fast!

otherwise taking care of him or her.) Newborns are a little intimidating, though, and the last thing you want is for anyone to think you're uncomfortable or ill-equipped to embrace your auntiehood from day one. Besides, being a Savvy Auntie is your birthright. Just as having a Savvy Auntie is your newborn niece's or nephew's birthright, too.

So consider this chapter's how-to tutorials our little secret. Practice the moves and heed the advice contained herein, and by the time you meet the little one, you'll be an old pro.

## Hand-le with Care

Auntie, I know how badly you want to snatch that little baby up and hold him or her oh-so-tightly. But please wash your hands first, with soap, for at least fifteen seconds of thorough scrubbing. Newborns are highly susceptible to germs, especially during their first month.

Also, don't go near your niece or nephew if you're sick. Newborns who develop a fever of 100.4 or more are required by law to go to the hospital, and what a totally unsavvy, unfortunate circumstance that would be.

# You Gotta Know How to Hold 'Em...

There are a few common positions most folks use to hold a baby, which I'll describe for right-handed aunties. Lefty aunties, do the opposite.

## The Cradle Hold

I suggest trying this one while seated, at least to start, allowing you to rest your arms comfortably in your lap while your newborn niece or nephew rests in your arms. (Also, it's OK to practice on a doll first, Auntie!)

1. When the baby is passed to you (often called "the handoff"), extend your right palm under the head and your left hand up between the legs and under the tush. Do the same when taking a baby out of a crib or bassinet; lift the head in your right hand, the tush in your left.

2. Reposition the baby so that the head rests in the crook of your right elbow, her back lies along your right forearm, and the tush becomes supported by your right hand. Do this by bringing your arms close to your chest as if you were going to cross them; your left hand will naturally slide out from under the baby's butt and up along your right arm. Your right hand is now in a perfect position to support the tush, while you use your left to prop the baby's head in the crook of your right arm.

3. You can then either position your left arm underneath your right to support it, or use your left hand to straighten the baby's little hat, gently fix the receiving blanket, or wipe away your own proud auntie tears.

4. If you have twin newborns and want to hold them simultaneously (Grandpa's taking a photo!), sit down and let someone place the babies in your arms. Be proud of all that precious arm candy, Auntie!

## The Over-the-Shoulder Hold

1. Drape a cloth diaper or spit-up towel over your shoulder, so that your memories of baby's first day don't include a stain on your favorite shirt.

2. Once again taking baby's head in one hand and tush in another, gently bring her up to meet your shoulder. You can continue to support her head in your hand, or simply let it rest sideways against the front of your shoulder.

3. Experiment with this hold to find what's most comfortable for baby and auntie; right-handed aunties, for example, might find it easier to hold the baby against their left shoulders, and vice versa. Once you have a little practice with this move (and the baby's old enough to support her head on her own), you can use your free hand to tap her tush ('cause that's just fun) or rub her back for a little extra TLC.

## The Belly Hold

Sometimes a baby will fuss in the cradle hold. The over-the-shoulder baby hold won't calm him either. That's when the belly hold comes into play. It's also useful for babies who need a burp.

1. Scoop the baby under his tummy and hold him facing down on your forearm, his head resting sideways in your hand.

2. If he's fussing, place your other arm along his back to keep him in place.

## Wee Recommend . . .

When changing your newborn nephew, try taking a second, clean diaper and holding it above his penis until his fresh diaper's securely in place. Boys have been known to wee-wee upward while on the changing table.

You've been warned.

# Know How to Fold 'Em ...

The second-most-daunting task you'll face as a new auntie will likely be diaper duty (or doody, I should say). Changing a newborn's nappy can be tricky, as even the tiniest of diapers seem to overwhelm a baby butt. But with a little nip and tuck, that baby will be ready to go (again).

1. Before you start, always wash your hands; do so again once you're done. Use hand sanitizer as a backup.

2. Gently lay your niece or nephew faceup on the changing table. Unfasten the sticky tabs around baby's hips to remove the dirty diaper. (Most folks like to gently lift a baby by the ankles, raising the tush a couple inches off the changing surface, then scooting the soiled diaper out from underneath.)

3. Wipe! Make sure there's no poop on the inner thighs or in the crevices of your baby niece's labia.

4. Lift by the ankles again to lay a fresh, open diaper under the tush. (The side of the diaper that's got those sticky fasteners is the side you're sliding under baby's bottom.)

5. Before fastening, make sure the tush and private parts are dry. Some parents will also use rash ointment or petroleum jelly to prevent diaper rash.

6. At this point, by the way, the baby's probably screaming. She's just cold, so work quickly! Try distracting her with a game of peekaboo or a loving smile.

7. Finish by folding the diaper up over the belly, exposing the sticky parts of the fasteners and affixing them to the special fastening panel on the front of the diaper. If the umbilical cord stump is still hanging around, don't cover it; fold down the waistband if needed. Leaving the stump exposed to air will help it dry up and fall off.

# Know When to Walk Away, Know When to Run

Just kidding—Savvy Aunties don't run from a crying baby! That would mean giving up precious auntie time and may give off the impression that you're some kind of newborn repellent.

But at some point, your newborn niece or nephew will cry in your arms. So think fast! Here are seven possible causes for a newborn's crying jag:

1. **The baby's chilly.**

   Newborns, you see, are used to being in Mama's ninety-eight-degree oven. Check that your own hands are warm and bring that newborn as close to your body as possible. (Skin to skin is best.) Snuggle and cuddle to re-create a womblike feeling. Bringing the baby close to your heart so she can hear your heartbeat is soothing, as is swaddling the baby in her receiving blanket (which, by

## HOW TO SWADDLE A BABY

Swaddling re-creates the cozy feeling of Mommy's womb and helps calm rattled baby nerves. Unfortunately, mastering good swaddling technique may rattle Auntie's nerves, because it does take practice. Here's how you do it.

STEP 1: Spread out the receiving blanket on a bed, changing table, or other large, soft surface.

STEP 2: Turn down the top right corner of the blanket about six inches.

STEP 3: Place the baby on the blanket at a diagonal so that her head is positioned right above that folded corner, her shoulders level with the folded edge.

STEP 4: Draw the right side of the blanket across baby's chest, pinning her left arm snugly against her, and tuck it tightly under baby's right side.

STEP 5: Bring the bottom of the blanket up toward the baby's body so that there's a snug fold around her feet. Depending on the blanket's size, you may need to tuck any extra fabric into the half swaddle you created in Step 4.

STEP 6: Now draw the left corner of the blanket across the baby's chest, securing her right arm, and tuck it tightly under the baby's left side.

Voilà. A handmade baby burrito!

the way, is just another word for a baby-sized blanket, one that's soft, breathable, and good for holding and swaddling).

2. The baby's uncomfortable.

The slightest thing can set off a baby: a twisted blanket, a diaper sticking to a patch of skin. Are you wearing something that might feel itchy against baby's skin? Did a loose hair of yours get wrapped around a tiny finger or toe? (That's called a hair tourniquet, and it's not as uncommon as it may seem.) Did the baby just eat? Babies swallow air when they feed. They also swallow air when they cry. All that air makes them gassy, which makes them cry some more. So maybe the problem is . . .

> **AUNTIEPEDIA: HAPPY SPITTER** A newborn who spits up a lot. It can look like your niece or nephew just spit up her or his entire meal, but that's just because saliva's coming up, too. Although it can be messy and worrisome, there's nothing medically wrong with being a happy spitter.
>
> AS IN: "Remember my stunning new silk blouse? It fell victim to the cutest happy spitter you ever did see."

3. The baby needs to burp.

Burping can be a frustrating process, because babies won't always do it on demand, even when it's in their best interest. But when they do let one go–whew! Relief for babies and aunties.

First, help prevent gas buildup by holding your niece or nephew upright during bottle feedings, so that less air gets swallowed. Burp after every two or three ounces of fluid; baby bottles are marked like measuring cups so you can tell how much the baby has had. (Mommies practice this by burping their babies when they switch breasts during feedings.) As the bottle nears empty, make sure the baby is taking in fluid, not air, by keeping the bottle pointed downward and the baby positioned upright.

When the meal's over, it's time for a final burp. Make sure you have a cloth diaper to cover yourself in case the baby spits up. There are three burping positions that work well:

❋ Burping position #1: Cupping the baby's chin between thumb and index finger (and using the heel of that hand to support the baby's chest), lean the baby slightly downward and, very gently, rub and pat her back with your other hand.

❋ Burping position #2: Put a cloth diaper over your shoulder and hold the baby against your

# *Auntie Up!* Ever Commit an Auntie-Oops?

**Aunties, even savvy ones, do make mistakes. Consider yourself gaffe-prone? Read our list of Auntie-Oopses below—and remember, you're in good company!**

*I gave peanut butter to my fifteen-month-old nephew several times over the course of a month. I didn't know kids weren't supposed to eat it until they were three. Oops!*

—Courtney Horn, Utica, OH

*I inadvertently drop F-bombs in front of my nephew. I can't keep the language clean!*

—Alisun Armstrong, New York, NY

*The first time I watched both my niece and nephew, I put my infant nephew's diaper on backwards. Afraid of being a bad aunt, I woke my two-year-old niece to check whether the picture on her diaper faced front or back. Their parents never knew.*

—Kim Oser, Washington, DC

*Do not put your face too close to a newborn after feeding them, particularly if they have a sensitive stomach. You may experience the taste of another human's . . . dinner.*

—Jennifer Iannolo, New York, NY

*I once leaned over my then-two-month-old nephew while I was adjusting him in his buggy, and I had this little purse hanging off my wrist. It swung a little and hit him in the face. He started to cry, although, luckily, he then stopped pretty quickly.*

—Daniella Topp, New York, NY

chest, her face looking out behind you. (See "The Over-the-Shoulder Hold" on page 88.) Again, gently rub and pat the baby's back until you hear a little belch.

❋ Burping position #3: Laying the baby facedown on your lap so that his head peeks over the side of one thigh, support the baby's upper body with your hand (like you did for Burping Position #1) and gently rub or pat the baby's back. Remember to keep the baby's head raised slightly above the rest of his body.

It may take five or ten minutes for a burp to come. It's also possible the baby won't burp at all. Don't worry. Just be sure to keep the baby upright for at least fifteen minutes after eating so air doesn't build up in the tummy. Try different burping positions during this time; if it still doesn't happen, keep the baby upright and try again a few minutes later.

4. **The baby's hungry.**

Inside the womb, a baby never had to ask for food, as Mommy's placenta smorgasbord stayed open for business 24/7. Now all of a sudden, your niece or nephew needs to call over a waiter and order milk. MILK! FEED ME! HELLO!?! CAN'T YOU TELL I'M HUNGRY? Even the most placid newborn can get his diaper in a twist when he's hungry.

A baby who's begun breast feeding may already know how to show he's hungry. Don't be shocked if your little nephew cocks his head toward your chest and opens his mouth longingly for your nipple. You may not smell like Mommy, but baby will take what he can get! Since your kitchen's closed, suggest that Mom take the baby back. If she's not available, grab a bottle of formula or Mommy's prepumped milk. However, I highly suggest speaking with Mom before ever feeding the baby on your own. There's a biological urge for mothers to feed their babies, so it may upset her that you are interrupting that bonding time. Plus, Mom's breasts may be filled to the brim, so breast feeding will help relieve her own pain and swelling. Only feed a baby with Mom's permission.

Once you've got the go-ahead, make sure to feed the baby only as much as the doctor has recommended for a single feeding. Otherwise you risk a throw-up situation. If it appears that your niece or nephew wants to keep on sucking after ingesting the allotted amount, give her or him a pacifier, if Mom and Dad have decided to use one. Otherwise, one of auntie's clean fingers will do in a pinch.

5. **The baby's gotta poop.**

What goes in must come out, so here's the scoop on poop.

First of all, babies do poop in the womb. That poop comes in a lovely shade of greenish black and is called meconium. A baby may continue to pass meconium in the first few days after birth.

The next type of poop, which you'll come to know well during the first month of diaper changing, is known as transition stool and can look bright yellowish-green, dark brown-green, or anything in between. Because it's more like fluid than stool, you might worry it's diarrhea, but that's just what newborn poop looks like. (In fact, until the baby starts eating solid food, poop is always gonna be on the liquidy side.)

Breast-fed babies poop differently than formula-fed babies. The poop of a breast-fed baby may look full of little seeds. It's kind of mustardy in color, and some say it smells a bit like sour milk (which is what it is, really). Formula-based poop is said to look more like a brownish peanut butter and to smell like, well, poop. Since the chemical composition of breast milk changes during infancy, a breast-fed baby's poop will also change, while formula-fed babies generally poop the same until they're eating solid food.

Breast-fed babies poop about eight to ten times a day in their first month, compared to about five times per day for formula-fed babies. That's because Mommy's milk contains colostrum, which is thought to act like a laxative. On the other hand, formula-fed babies are more likely to experience constipation.

Once your baby niece or nephew is about two months old, pooping will reduce to once a day or so, although some babies can go for days without a poop. However, anytime your niece or nephew seems uncomfortable—and you've ruled out the other possible causes we've discussed—the problem might be constipation.

What can you do to help? Bend the baby's knees toward his chest to help him push the poop out, move his legs around in a cycling motion to loosen things up, or massage the baby's tummy in a warm bath.

If constipation becomes a persistent problem, Mom might consider adding a little more water to a baby's formula, or she can ask the pediatrician if glycerin suppositories are appropriate.

6. The baby's overstimulated.

Wow, what a lucky baby! So many people want to play with him! And hold him! And sing to him! Give him teddy bears! Pose for pics with him! Play peekaboo with him! It's all so much fun!

Until it's not. Look, that newborn was pretty comfy in the womb. And frankly, except for the fact that his lease was up, he would've been quite content to stay in there even longer. Now all this real-world stuff is too much to handle: The people! The paparazzi! The lights! Baby can't take it anymore!

*Waaaaaaaaaaaaaaaaa!!!*

Crying is one way a baby lets you know that it's time to go into a dark room and relax. (Don't worry about quiet, though. You can talk in a normal voice around a sleeping newborn.)

Other signs that the baby's calling a time-out:

❋ Closing his eyes, shielding himself from the lights and action around him.

❋ Turning away from you and all the goings-on.

❋ Emitting angry cries: "I said enough is enough, Auntie! Too much stimulation!"

Swaddling the baby (see #1 above) will help.

7. The baby's a baby.

Here's the thing, Auntie. No matter how savvy you are, there will be times when the baby cries and you won't know why. You will have tried everything we've mentioned here, plus taken advice from other aunties and great-aunties, and still be at a loss.

Sometimes, babies cry. It's what they do. In fact, babies who cry a lot are called colicky. Babies have colic when they cry for more than three hours every day, for more than three days a week, for more than three weeks in a row. And hardly anything soothes them for longer than a few minutes at a time. (Swaddling and massaging are often thought to help, though. See swaddling above or baby massage below.)

No study has been able to show why some babies are colicky and others aren't. It's just as common in boys as it is in girls. Breast-fed babies are as likely to have colic as formula-fed babies. Bald babies, hairy babies, big babies, little babies, firstborn babies, twin babies, single babies– they can all experience colic. It generally starts about two weeks after the baby is born and lasts until the baby is about three or four months old.

And yes, it can be exhausting. So if your niece or nephew has colic, try to be there for the parents as much as you can in those first few months. They will seriously need the relief.

# Bath Time!

I've saved the best for last, because take it from me—there's nothing better than giving your newborn niece or nephew a bath. They're so happy in there, so content . . . it's like how an auntie feels when she's at the spa.

I also know how petrifying it is to give a newborn a bath for the first time. And no offense, Auntie, but your niece or nephew is a little nervous about this whole production, too. Let me assure you, though, that you are not going to drown the baby. Here's what you will do.

Fill the baby's sink tub with just enough lukewarm water to cover her butt while you've got her in there, head held up, in a seated position. Hold her securely; I like to wrap an arm around the baby's torso. With a soft baby cloth, wipe from the top down; since the dirtiest parts are on bottom, you'll be using cleaner water to wash her head, face, neck and chest. Wash the private parts extra gently.

Although there are some adorably tempting baby body washes on the market, you can just use water. If the parents prefer soap, fragrance-free is best. And honestly, no need for a bubble bath until the baby's old enough to ask for one.

Shampooing is also unnecessary, unless the baby's got cradle cap (dry, scaly skin on the top of his head). If you like, a tiny drop of a very mild, gentle baby shampoo will do. Rinse the hair with a cup of clean water, or lukewarm water straight from the faucet.

After bath time, lay your niece or nephew down on the changing table or a soft surface like a bed and gently pat dry with a soft towel. A completely dry baby is very important to prevent diaper rash or other unpleasant skin conditions.

# Baby Massaging

One more thing before you're done, Auntie. Studies demonstrate that a baby massage can improve your niece's or nephew's digestion and sleep patterns; many parents also swear it's the only way to soothe a colicky baby. If your niece or nephew is a preemie, a baby massage three times a day for the first week or two has been shown to promote growth and development faster than if premature newborns don't receive massages.

It's not necessary to use lotion—but if you do, don't use it anywhere near the genitalia, as rashes will be more likely to spring up. Instead, you may want to consider just a drop of baby oil.

Besides doing it with a little TLC, there's no "best" method of baby massage. I suggest you start by gently rubbing your clean, dry hands on baby's head in a circular motion. Then add a drop of oil and massage the chest, arms, and legs in gentle, circular motions. Most babies will enjoy this, but if your niece or nephew seems put off by it, don't force it. There's nothing like a bad massage.

Turn the baby over to massage the back and shoulders. The whole massage should last about two to five minutes, depending on the baby's temperament. Dab off the oil with a towel. Last step—lots of kisses!

# Quick Fixer-Uppers

Here are a few more areas where newborns need a little upkeep.

## Diaper Rash

LOOKS LIKE: Red, irritated skin around the tush, genitals, and thighs; inflamed penis; ammonia smell; discomfort during diaper changes.

THE REMEDY: Change the diaper more often. Make sure the baby's bottom is completely dry and aired out before putting on a new nappy. Gently rub zinc oxide, lanolin ointment, or petroleum jelly onto the rash. On doctor's orders, apply antifungal cream. (Diaper rash is often caused by *Candida,* a kind of yeast infection that may pop up if a niece or nephew was recently on antibiotics.)

## Teething

LOOKS LIKE: Little baby teeth coming in! Except not always. Before teeth actually surface, you may see your niece or nephew drooling and coughing a lot, as teething stimulates saliva production. She or he may also gnaw and bite as a means of self-soothing.

THE REMEDY: Give the baby a cold, wet cloth to bite down on. If you want to use a teething ring, the American Academy of Pediatrics recommends rubbery ones with some give, not hard or frozen ones. Sometimes sucking on an auntie's finger is a niece's or nephew's favorite kind of relief. (Wash your hands first!)

## Nail-clipping

LOOKS LIKE: A really annoying paper cut on your cheek. Baby nails are like ridiculous little machetes! And they grow insanely fast.

THE REMEDY: Using specially made baby nail clippers or scissors, give a mini mani/pedi—while the baby's asleep so there's no fussing. Gently push baby's finger pads away from the nail tips, then snip. Alternatively, use the soft side of an emery board to file nails down.

# The Not-so-Adorable Truth About Newborns

When a Savvy Auntie cradles that little angel in her arms for the very first time, she marvels at how instantly she's fallen in love. She thinks about how her life will never be the same. And sometimes, she can't help wondering, "Do all newborn babies look like this?"

One of the dirty little secrets of delivery is that many babies come out looking less than beatific. It can take a few days or even a few months for the irresistible cuteness to set in, but don't worry. It will! In the meantime, Dr. Stephanie Lichten, a pediatric hospitalist at Jacobi Medical Center in Bronx, New York, serves up a helping of, "What's up with this baby?"

## Why do newborns have such bad skin?

A brand-new baby just got kicked out of the nice, warm, moist womb, and suddenly his or her epidermis is subjected to nothing but dry air. Just think about what that would do to your complexion! In the first through third weeks of life, your nephew's or niece's skin will begin to flake and peel. If the skin's badly cracked, plain old petroleum jelly should do the trick.

About half of all newborns develop acne, either typical red blemishes or tiny white bumps caused by blocked pores called milia. (Yeah, adults get those, too.) It's caused by the transfer of hormones from Mom to baby prior to delivery. A case of baby acne usually resolves itself within the first six months.

Blisters are a different story. If you see them or find signs of blood or pus, get over the yuck factor and bring it to the parents' attention right away.

## What are birthmarks? Are they always permanent?

Mongolian spots are bluish-gray, flat marks that look like little bruises and usually show up on baby's bum. Most fade by two or three years of age. Capillary hemangiomas are more commonly (and cutely) called "stork bites and angel kisses." These are flat, pinkish marks usually spotted at the nape of the neck (stork bites) or around the forehead and eyes (angel kisses). Most fade within the first two years of life. Those on the neck may persist into adulthood, but once your niece's or nephew's hairline fills in, they'll stay camouflaged.

*Why do some babies come out looking like hairy little monkeys?*

Some babies are born with a lot of hair—and not just on their head. Lanugo, the technical term for that soft body hair, is much more common in preemies and serves as a protective covering to help them stay warm. Expect the big shedding season to occur within the first month.

*How long does the umbilical stump stick around? Do I have to do anything with it?*

It usually falls off within the first two weeks; if it's still hanging on after three, consult a pediatrician. Unpleasant though it may be, you should swab the base of the stump twice daily with alcohol and make sure it's exposed to dry air throughout the day to encourage it to shrivel up and fall off. Fold over the front band of the baby's diaper so the cord won't get stuck underneath in moisture-retaining Diaper Rash Land.

*Exactly how soft and vulnerable is a newborn's skull?*

Newborns have two "soft spots," a.k.a. fontanel, on their heads. A very small one in the back usually closes within the first few months. The larger, anterior fontanel—what people are usually talking about when they say "the soft spot"—closes around fifteen to eighteen months. Why so long? To allow the baby's brain to grow rapidly. You'll notice how much your little one learns in the first year of life!

*How are things supposed to look, you know, down there?*

In baby boys, you may notice swelling around the scrotum. This is called hydrocele and is nothing but plain and simple fluid retention. (See, you and your nephew already have something in common. Occasional bloating!) It usually resolves itself between nine and twelve months. Swelling can sometimes be a sign of a hernia, especially if you can only see it along one side of the baby's lower abdomen. Contrary to rumor, a baby's hernia doesn't cause a red or blue discoloration and isn't hard or painful. In fact, it can be taken care of rather easily with gentle pressure.

If a boy is circumcised, usually his penis will be swollen and a little tender for the first few days. Monitor it for increased redness or even a bit of blood (which are both normal) and treat these with some Bacitracin, Neosporin, and Auntie's TLC.

Girls may have swollen labia and/or some vaginal discharge, all very common, caused by the passage of maternal hormones from Mom to baby during birth. It may last about six weeks, longer in breast-fed babies.

### *What's up with all the spitting?*

Spitting up, a.k.a. reflux, occurs in almost all babies during the first six months of life. The muscle that controls the passage of food from the esophagus into the stomach isn't mature enough yet to do its job, so stuff winds up going back up and out the mouth. You can lessen spit-ups by feeding the baby little bits at a time and holding the baby upright during feeding. (See the information on burping positions, on pages 91, 93.) By six months, babies' muscle development allows stomach closure to work properly, so reflux is no longer a problem.

### *I've heard that newborns are blind during their first two weeks of life. Is this true? And why does this one look all cross-eyed?*

Newbies do have poor vision (approximately 20/400), but they can process shades. Around two weeks of age they will begin to fix their gaze—and lucky you, studies show they love staring at adults' faces most of all! It may take until six months before a baby develops a conjugate gaze, when both eyes can focus in the same direction. And 20/20 vision? Although your niece or nephew may already be practically perfect in every way, perfect vision doesn't develop until about six years of age.

### *I think the little boo is smiling at me. Is the little boo smiling at me?*

Babies smile with purpose (known as a social smile) starting at two months. You'll be able to engage and entertain your niece or nephew at this point, and she or he will give you the most precious looks in return! Some babies do have a social smile as early as six weeks of age, but any smiles prior to that are most likely just gas.

# Love at First Sight . . . Or Not

We're supposed to fall madly in love with a niece or nephew from the moment we lay eyes on her or him, right? So if you're not feeling that way, does that mean you've got a heart of stone?

No! In fact, Natalie Robinson Garfield, psychotherapist and author of *The Sense Connection: Discovering How Your Five Senses Determine Your Effectiveness as a Person, Partner, and Parent,* says, "Don't expect love at first sight." Instead, "enjoy the 'getting to know you' process." To increase your love connection, provide your niece or nephew with as much hands-on caregiving as you can. (That's right; you can diaper your way to pure adoration!)

Here's a deep secret nobody ever talks about: new mothers feel this way quite frequently. Sometimes it's because a difficult delivery didn't let them bond with the baby at the very start. Sometimes it's just because, hey, newborns are strangers, too. It takes time for everyone to adjust. Relax and it will happen.

*OK, I swear, now the baby's out-and-out flirting with me. But I must be imagining that, right?*

He or she just might be flirting with you. In her book *Woman: An Intimate Geography,* Pulitzer Prize–winning science writer Natalie Angier describes how boys and girls age four and under are more sexual than their older, grade-school siblings, who have entered sexual latency and remain asexual until puberty. It's because babies still have a lot of reproductive hormones in their systems left over from delivery (which only gets under way once Mom's bod starts churning boatloads of hormones).

This means babies may also be more sexual with themselves. Don't be too freaked out if you see your young niece or nephew touching herself or himself. (You can be a little freaked out, just not a lot.)

# Baby Parenting Secrets, Revealed!

Do Mom and Dad seem to have a sixth sense for keeping your newborn niece or nephew calm, content, and cry-free? Please don't assume that parenthood has bestowed upon them magical powers that you, as an auntie, could never possess. Chances are they've had help from a parenting guru. (A quick glance at any books on their nightstands will probably prove it.)

Being a parent is a hard job, which is why some of them like to embrace a particular parenting philosophy like the ones I've listed below. As Savvy Aunties, we give props to the parents who take charge while trying to give their kids the best upbringing possible. If reading a child-care expert's book and following some of his or her techniques can help calm a colicky baby at 3:00 A.M. or result in more productive feedings, why not? (Research has also shown that children with well-regulated sleep and naptimes enjoy better cognitive development down the road.) Whether that means "Ferberizing," "banguage," or "babywearing," parents should raise their kids as they see fit (as long as they're raising them in a safe environment, of course).

Some parents may take these guidelines as gospel, even judging others for not adopting the same methods. Some will borrow from different philosophies, creating a unique approach that works for them. As a Savvy Auntie, your job is simply to be aware of what these different methods entail and to acquire the expertise needed to support Mom and Dad's choices.

What if your niece's or nephew's parents seem to be winging it, paying the price in frazzled days and sleepless nights? Try suggesting one of the following books, or attempt a new putting-baby-to-bed routine the next time you babysit. Watch as Mom and Dad gawk in amazement at your auntuition!

**METHOD**

Ferberizing

**GURU**

Dr. Richard Ferber, director of Boston's Center for Pediatric Sleep Disorders

**BOOK**

*Solve Your Child's Sleep Problems*

**PHILOSOPHY**

Encourage "gradual extinction" of middle-of-the-night crying jags by incrementally delaying your response to a baby's sobs, thus allowing the child to "self-soothe."

## Savvy Auntie's Role

If you're taking care of your niece or nephew and she or he wakes up crying, follow Mom and Dad's Ferberizing instructions, no matter how tough it is to listen to that little angel cry. (You'll usually only have to hang back for a few minutes, tops.)

**METHOD**

Mindell Method

**GURU**

Clinical psychologist Jodi Mindell, associate director of the Sleep Disorders Center at the Children's Hospital of Philadelphia

**BOOK**

*Sleeping Through the Night: How Infants, Toddlers, and Their Parents Can Get a Good Night's Sleep*

**PHILOSOPHY**

Focus on bedtime rituals (rather than what to do in the middle of the night) to ensure healthy sleep, such as putting babies down while they're still awake.

## Savvy Auntie's Role

If Mom and Dad have a going-to-bed ritual, learn it and stick to it. I know nobody wants to close the nursery door on a baby who's still awake, so be strict with yourself if you must!

**METHOD**

Baby whispering

**GURU**

Tracy Hogg, RNMH, a British-born nurse, midwife, and celebrity nanny

**BOOK**

*Secrets of the Baby Whisperer: How to Calm, Connect, and Communicate with Your Baby*

**PHILOSOPHY**

By learning to interpret "banguage"—that is, baby language, or the signals babies give off when they're unhappy—a caregiver can best respond to baby's needs. That may sound New Age-y, but Hogg's recommendations are actually pretty old-school, like keeping infants on strict sleeping and feeding schedules.

## Savvy Auntie's Role

You'll definitely want to learn how to read banguage. (It sounds kinda fun, no?) When it's your turn to babysit, have the sleeping and feeding routines down cold.

**METHOD**

Karp Method

**GURU**

Dr. Harvey Karp, assistant professor of pediatrics at UCLA School of Medicine

**BOOK**

*The Baby Book: Everything You Need to Know About Your Baby from Birth to Age Two*

**PHILOSOPHY**

Babies leave the womb three months too soon, thus causing all the common problems associated with newborns. To reduce babies' stress and pave the way for happy development, simulate the womb environment using the five S's: swaddling, side/stomach position, *shhh* sounds, swinging, and sucking.

## Savvy Auntie's Role

Learn how to swaddle (see page 90). The other S's aren't as tough to master but, of course, should also be adhered to.

**METHOD**

Weissbluth Method

**GURU**

Dr. Marc Weissbluth, founder of the Sleep Disorders Center at Chicago's Children's Memorial Hospital

**BOOK**

*Healthy Sleep Habits, Happy Child*

**PHILOSOPHY**

Since sleep-deprived babies lose out on beneficial physical and cognitive development in the long run, parents should learn how to observe and follow their child's natural sleeping patterns for best results. (However, regularly scheduled naps are also a big tenet here.)

## Savvy Auntie's Role

If your niece or nephew has a naptime, stick to it! By helping to keep the baby on a regular sleep cycle, you'll also be saving the parents future sleepless nights.

# What's Your Sign, Baby?

Since babies' hand-eye coordination develops faster than their verbal skills, using sign language to communicate with them has become a very popular parenting practice. (It's a method that's not associated with any one baby guru, so there are many books on the subject to choose from.) Studies have shown that babies who sign tend to be happier and less frustrated. Teaching begins at about six months of age; by the eighth or ninth month, babies can sign for things like more milk or their favorite toy.

### METHOD
Attachment parenting

### GURU
Dr. William Sears, associate clinical professor of pediatrics at University of California–Irvine

### BOOK
*The Happiest Baby on the Block: The New Way to Calm Crying and Help Your Newborn Baby Sleep Longer*

### PHILOSOPHY
Babies develop better with secure parental attachments, both physical and emotional, which include babywearing (carrying the baby in a cloth sling that fits snugly against the parent's body) and cosleeping (sleeping in the same bed as Mom and Dad, starting at birth). The American Academy of Pediatrics and the Consumer Product Safety Commission have come out against cosleeping, saying it may cause SIDS if a parent mistakenly rolls over onto a baby in bed. However, there are cosleepers on the market (see "Newbornzzz" on page 63) designed to make cosleeping safer.

## Savvy Auntie's Role
Although you may want to try on that babywearing sling, it's only meant to be worn by the parents, so best not to interfere. Same goes for sharing your bed with a baby.

❋

## METHOD

The "no-cry" method

### GURU

Parent educator Elizabeth Pantley

### BOOK

*The No-Cry Sleep Solution: Gentle Ways to Help Your Baby Sleep Through the Night*

### PHILOSOPHY

Soothe a crying baby immediately. An infant's sleep patterns should be analyzed by the parents, but parents should also have lots of leeway in picking the child-rearing methods that work best for them (cosleeping, breast or bottle feeding, etc.).

## *Savvy Auntie's Role*

As soon as you hear that baby crying, go soothe her until she falls back asleep in your arms.

## METHOD

Elimination Communication

### GURU

Ingrid Bauer, an author and speaker on parenting and natural living

### BOOK

*Diaper Free: The Gentle Wisdom of Natural Infant Hygiene*

### PHILOSOPHY

Parents can recognize when a baby needs to go potty by learning certain cues, signals, and intuitions, thus cutting down on diaper rash, diaper cost, and landfill waste. (The philosophy is based on Bauer's travels in less industrialized countries, where disposable diapers are rare.)

## *Savvy Auntie's Role*

Newborns go (number one and number two) many, many times a day. Parents who are trying to get the hang of elimination communication could use some patient vibes sent their way, not to mention help cleaning up any "miscommunications."

# Baby Blues or Postpartum Depression?

Most moms feel down after giving birth. Sometimes it's a case of the baby blues–the unofficial but widely used term for a temporary spell of sadness and mood swings–and sometimes it's a more serious, long-term case of postpartum depression (PPD), which is considered a clinical disorder and requires professional help.

Aunties who spend time with Mom in the days and weeks after birth should be on the lookout for signs of either one.

|  | BABY BLUES | POSTPARTUM DEPRESSION |
|---|---|---|
| When may it occur? | About four days after giving birth | About two weeks after birth (but usually starts as baby blues) |
| How long might she feel this way? | About ten days | Can last for months if left untreated |
| What causes it? | Sleep deprivation and hormonal changes | Same as baby blues. A personal or family history of depression increases the likelihood of PPD; in addition, a 2010 survey by *Baby Talk* magazine noted a possible correlation between having a C-section and later experiencing PPD. |
| What are the symptoms? | Irritability, tears, insomnia, mood swings, feeling overwhelmed | All of the preceding, plus withdrawal, trouble focusing, or too much or too little sleep, to the point where Mom can't properly care for herself or her baby |
| How common is it? | About 50-75 percent of American women report having baby blues symptoms | About 10 percent of American women |
| How can I help? | Be understanding. Watch the baby so she can nap or shower. | Do house chores for her. Don't judge. Make sure she seeks treatment and gets on medication. Make a doctor's appointment yourself and drive her there if needed. |

Sadly, 1 in 1,000 new mothers suffer from a worst-case-scenario of postpartum psychosis. Usually, women with a history of bipolar or schizoaffective disorder are at a higher risk for it. Symptoms may start showing around six weeks after childbirth and include delusions, hallucinations, obsessive thoughts, and rapid mood swings. If you think someone is exhibiting these symptoms, seek medical attention immediately.

## Postpartum Pop?

A study published in the *Journal of the American Medical Association* reported that 14 percent of new dads experience some form of depression about three to six months after a child is born. The study also found that new dads and expectant dads have twice the level of depression as the rest of the adult-male population, and that "there is a clear and consistent link between father's depression and mother's depression." In other words, baby blues may be contagious.

# Relying on Auntuition:
# Ten Steps to the Art of Auntie-ing

As you grow into your Savvy Auntie status, caring for your nieces and nephews will start to feel like second nature. What's great is knowing that your instinctual urges—those delicious desires to hug, kiss, and cuddle a newborn as well as the strong pull you feel inside you when the baby cries—are what's guiding you toward better and better auntie-ing skills. This is stuff that you probably don't need a book to teach you. But it's also some of the best stuff about auntie-ing, so I couldn't help sharing.

1. Affectionate, loving touch is essential for developing newborns' brains and bodies. Science has shown that preemies develop more quickly when caressed, and babies tend to cry less when held.

2. Responding to a baby's or young child's needs makes him or her feel secure, and a secure child grows up to be a secure adult. So put down that BlackBerry when caring for your niece or nephew and focus on what she or he needs. Watch for signals and read between the cries.

3. No matter how deep the discussion you're having with an uncle, if a toddler is grabbing for your attention, give it to him. Your responsiveness will make the child feel secure.

4. Address a child's needs with warmth and timeliness. This will build trust.

5. Stimulate children's minds with new activities. Studies have shown that opening up a little one to a new experience, game, or toy can actually demonstrate brain growth within hours.

6. On the other hand, don't overstimulate them with too many toys or games at once. For little ones, play is work, so imagine what it would be like if the assignments kept piling up on your desk. That's how your niece is feeling when she starts to cry, surrounded by all the new toys you just bought her. Try one toy at a time, and let her explore the toy the way she wants to. If she appears frustrated, you can lead the way by talking through the solution and slowly showing her how it works.

7. Give the child attention. Despite what we used to think, you can't actually spoil a child with too much attention. They ask for what they need (including hugs!).

8. No matter how bad your day at work, it's best not to let it show around the little ones. Even babies can feel tension. If they're exposed to their parents' stress, offer to take them for a walk.

9. It's tough to give multiple nieces and nephews all the attention they need all the time. Do the best you can.

10. Take care of yourself. After a long visit, you may need a nap or a cocktail. Consider these your self-administered pats on the back for helping the most important little people in your life to grow up as best they can.

# Oh, the Stages They'll Grow!

Watching your newborn niece or nephew grow up is one of the most special privileges of being a Savvy Auntie, especially during baby's first year, which is chock-full of so many adorable changes. Check out this timeline to find out what'll happen when. (But do note, Auntie: Every baby develops in her or his own good time. Don't worry if your niece or nephew doesn't follow this list to the moment. Also, preemies do start a bit behind but tend to catch up by two years of age.)

**2 WEEKS:** Baby can hold a brief gaze. Starts to lift head when lying facedown.

**1 MONTH:** If you're a foot or so away, he or she will hold your gaze, but only for a few moments. Can also shake head "no" side to side. Only a month old and already acting like a sullen teenager!

**2 MONTHS:** Smiles! Lots of oohs and aahs! Can track movement (say, a toy train) by sight.

**3 MONTHS:** "Hey, wait a minute," baby's expression seems to say. "Not only can I see Auntie's face . . . I actually recognize it, having seen it before! And since I can now see color, I can see her gorgeous green eyes!" Baby may then acknowledge said recognition by opening and closing fingers to approximate a wave, which then develops into grasping and reaching for things thanks to newfound hand-eye coordination. (Did she just pilfer your iPod? Yep.) Kicking up a storm. Starts to imitate vocal sounds.

**4 MONTHS:** Auntie, I know your niece or nephew is not a dog, but look at how nicely she or he sits (with the aid of some extra back support) and rolls over! Other big-kid feats include sleeping (almost) through the night. Lots of smiling and babbling. Begins exploring the world one object in mouth at a time. (Be vigilant about keeping choking hazards far away!) Teething may start because, as baby will learn, it's always something.

**5 MONTHS:** Baby can see you from all the way across the room: Auntie's here! Auntie's here! Notices your jewelry and other small objects–pretty! shiny!–and grabs them for an up-close inspection.

**6 MONTHS:** He's sitting all by himself! OK, he fell over. Let's try that again. Look, he's sitting all by himself! OK, he fell over again. Who cares, let's play monkey-see, monkey-do. Auntie smiles; baby smiles! Auntie makes a confused expression; baby makes a confused expression! We'll play more after our bottle, which baby can now hold solo and ask for out loud with a confident "baa baa."

**7 MONTHS:** Have you ever seen anything as amazing as your niece or nephew responding to the sound of her or his own name? Not only that, but this baby could set a new world record for hours spent playing nonstop peekaboo! That'll take strength, so let's eat! But can we call it eating when only one out of every bajillion peas actually makes it into his mouth? Oh, well, at least he's able to feed himself finger foods.

8 MONTHS: Peas still drop in massive quantities, but now baby does it on purpose for the sheer amusement. Auntie can try spoon-feeding for a better peas-to-mouth ratio, except baby can now grab that spoon and probably wants to chew on it more than the peas. Whew, Daddy just got home! Baby's been responding differently to different family members, but always reacts positively to Pop's presence, with lots of happy babbling. (Probably trying to explain to Dad how, thanks to falling peas, gravity was just discovered.) Pretty soon it's off to bed. Now this is sleeping like a baby. We're up to eleven to thirteen hours a night!

9 MONTHS: Who's the fairest of them all? Your niece, who just found herself in the mirror! Not to mention the nimblest of them all. Look at her picking up toys, and how she can go from lying on her tummy to sitting up.

10 MONTHS: How's this for a party trick? Baby can pull herself up to standing, and can stay standing if holding on to Auntie's hands! Other nifty stunts include passing objects from one hand to the other (juggling 101!) and, well, crying when objects are taken away. ("Hey, I was eating that sunglasses case!")

11 MONTHS: Mama! Dada! And if you're around frequently enough, just maybe a sound for you, Auntie! Baby's so proud of himself: Clap, clap, clap! And now he's waving good-bye. Aww!

1 YEAR: Happy birthday, baby! How about a special birthday lunch? Do you want peaches? Baby can shake her head as if to insist: "No! No peaches!" Later on, as the birthday star gets dolled up for her big party, dressing is easier than ever. She knows to extend her arms to get that sweater on. Mingling among the party guests like quite the social butterfly, baby crawls all over the place and "cruises" (which really is the official term for it) along the furniture, taking upright steps while holding on. Then it's time to take over the dance floor! Baby rocks that tush to the music. It might not be all fun and games on that momentous day, though. Your niece or nephew may be fearful of guests who haven't come around often. She or he also may not want to share all these new toys. In fact, let's try taking my cousin's dolly to see what happens. (Remember, Auntie: This is only a test.) After such an exhausting affair, a relaxing read before bed is definitely necessary. Good thing your one-year-old niece or nephew loves nothing more than an auntie-narrated bedtime story.

# Festivaunts 5

FROM THE VERY FIRST DAY you become an auntie, all the days that follow feel a little more special. But of course, some days—birthday, holidays, religious celebrations, family firsts, and commemorations—really *are* a little more special. And *special occasions always call for extra planning,* which just so happens to be a Savvy Auntie's specialty. Let the fetes begin!

# Religious Rituals and Observauntses

If your niece's or nephew's parents are religious, you've probably already heard about the bris, simchat bat, or baptism scheduled to take place after the baby's born. Then again, sometimes a momentous milestone like birth makes people seek out traditions in ways they didn't care about before. Don't be surprised if a nonpracticing parent suddenly insists on a ceremony! As an auntie, there are many meaningful ways you might participate and a few things you should know.

## For Jews

The brit milah (Hebrew for circumcision, often shortened to bris) is typically performed on the morning of the eighth day after birth and represents the covenant between God and the Jewish people. The ritual is performed by a mohel, a role often fulfilled by a moonlighting physician. (No matter what his day job, a mohel must always hold special certifications.) It may take place in a synagogue, at home, or wherever the parents prefer. During the bris, your nephew will be given his Jewish name.

Girls get a special occasion, too, a naming ceremony. Your niece may be given her Jewish name on a Monday, Thursday, Jewish holiday, or Sabbath day. While she probably won't be present at her minicoronation, she'll get to flaunt that new party dress you got her at her simchat bat ("celebration of a daughter") or shalom bat ("welcome the daughter"). Unlike the bris, your niece's naming ceremony can occur anytime during her first year of life.

### SAVVY AUNTIE'S ROLE

In the Ashkenazi tradition, the assignment to transfer the baby from mother to father before and after the bris is often bestowed upon a couple trying to have children. The sandek (usually a man with close ties to the family, like the uncle) holds the baby on his lap during the actual circumcision, which is considered the highest honor.

If you're helping plan the party, which is always a festive celebration replete with bagels, lox, and balloons, consider the location and whether you need to hire a kosher caterer. Once the fun is done, whatever postbris diaper changing you do for your nephew should adhere to any special instructions given by the mohel to avoid infection.

## For Christians

A baptism is the rite of passage by which a person becomes a member of the Christian church. As it involves a ritual washing, it also symbolizes cleansing from original sin (i.e., the whole Adam-and-Eve-eating-the-apple thing). Although a person can be baptized at any age, if your niece's or nephew's family is Christian, typically she or he is baptized within the first few months of life, inside of a church. The baby wears a white christening gown, signifying purity, and the minister/priest/bishop performs an aspersion, sprinkling your niece's or nephew's head with water drawn from the church's baptismal font.

As with a bris, there's typically an at-home party that follows. Guests may give your niece or nephew small presents or monetary gifts, and you can usually count on a nice big cake.

### SAVVY AUNTIE'S ROLE

Many of us became Savvy Aunties when a close friend or relative asked us to be a child's godmother. As far as the church is concerned, godparents "sponsor" a child's baptism. During the ceremony, the godparents (who needn't be a married couple or related to the baby) stand at the font with the priest and parents. You'll have a few lines to say, mostly of the "I will" and "We do" variety, as prompted by the clergy performing the ceremony.

Some families make it a tradition that the godmother purchases the baby's christening gown, but check on that with Mom before going shopping. (Sometimes christening gowns are held on to as heirlooms and passed down within the family.) It's also considered traditional for the godmother to gift her godchild with a small, religious keepsake, like a rosary, a Bible, or a statuette.

After the baptism, your godmotherly duties include ensuring that your niece or nephew receives a proper religious education, serving as her or his unofficial spiritual adviser, and stepping in to raise the child if she or he becomes orphaned. Although that's all considered pretty outdated by most modern families, it is often the case that the woman Mom and Dad pick as godmother also gets named the child's legal guardian in the parents' will.

## Signs Mom May Need Party-Planning Help

She just had another baby and probably can't imagine pulling off a party amid all the late-night breast feeding and dozen-times-daily diaper changes.

Recent mentions she's made of money being tight.

An extended family member recently took ill or passed away, probably dampening her enthusiasm for balloons and birthday cake.

Didn't we just throw a birthday party last month?

# Birthdays!

Who doesn't love a party? And when it's your niece's or nephew's birthday party, there's no place you'd rather be—even if you're just there long enough to leave a gift and watch her or him blow out the candles, and even if you've got to hop a plane to get there.

Sometimes aunties are asked to bake the cake or cupcakes for the birthday party. Sometimes they plan the whole event! Mom may be busy with other siblings, work, or whatever else is going on in her family's life. Or maybe planning parties just ain't her thing.

So let's say you're in charge, Auntie. Even if this is a one-year-old's birthday party (so special!), you can pull this off without going over budget or overstepping your bounds. In fact, what people often forget is that first birthday parties really shouldn't be huge bashes. (Honestly, less is more!) The guest of honor can't last long without a nap, can't open presents or eat cake without help, and doesn't even know what all the commotion is about. A few baby-age friends and family may be in attendance, but really this party is a reason for adults to get together for a fun, stress-free, memorable occasion. So use that savoir flair I know you've got, Auntie!

For help, I spoke with Lisa Kothari, kids' party expert and founder of Peppers and Pollywogs, a web-based company all about kids' parties.

**SIX WEEKS BEFORE**

**Choose theme.** Ask parents for input.

**Choose location.** Parents' place, your house? In backyard, basement, and so on?

**Finalize date/time.** Traditional weekend afternoon? Casual weekday dinner? Important—set a start *and* end time! Helps parents plan little ones' naps, meals, and so on. Two-hour party is ideal.

**Build guest list.** Work with Mom on it. Track down mailing addresses, surname spellings, and so on, as needed.

 **FOUR WEEKS BEFORE**

**Mail invitations**—snail mail, not e-mail! Paper invites are always more appropriate and appreciated. Try to buy or make ones that go with party's theme.

**Book entertainment,** if having any. Do you need to audition people first? See: Now That's Entertainment!

 **THREE WEEKS BEFORE**

**Place any online orders** for decorations, and so on. This allows time to make returns if needed.

**Start lining up help.** First round of recruits includes significant other, other Savvy Aunties. Divvy up baking duties, assign carpools for older relatives, convince child's favorite uncle to dress up in goofy costume.

**ONE TO TWO WEEKS BEFORE**

**Finalize guest list.** Follow up with any outstanding RSVPs.

**Decide on menu.** Keep it simple! Stick to kid-friendly foods. Pizza, chicken fingers? Cross-check guest list for allergy concerns.

**Decide on cake.** Ordering (if so, do now!) or making yourself? Find out birthday boy/girl's favorite flavors from Mom. See: Kiddie Cake Trends.

**Take inventory.** Got everything needed to decorate? Accessories for backyard games, and so on?

**Plan contents of goodie bags.** Very important! See: "From Goodie to Great" on page 122!

# Now That's Entertainment!

A few things to keep in mind when hiring b-day entertainment:

❋ Small kids may be frightened by a life-sized version of their favorite TV and movie characters. Let them know what to expect before a six-foot Barney arrives.

❋ Have a backup character or two in mind. A company may only have one Dora the Explorer.

❋ Keep cash on hand at the party; tips are often expected and always appreciated.

❋ Cartoon characters aren't the only kinds of entertainers! Consider jugglers, magicians, face painters, puppeteers, balloon-animal makers, storytellers, and so on. However . . .

❋ NO CLOWNS! You'll run the risk of scaring the poop out of a little kid. A 2007 study on the subject concluded that kids universally dislike clowns, probably because of their exaggerated, often-creepy facial expressions. And for that matter, no mimes, either.

# Kiddie Cake Trends Every Savvy Auntie Should Know

SMASH CAKE: A miniature replica of a child's birthday cake, measuring a few inches on each side, made especially for young birthday boys and girls who prefer destroying cake to eating it. Prevents an entire cake from getting ruined. Many supermarkets and bakeries that sell special-order birthday cakes will throw in a smash cake for free or cheap.

CUPCAKE CAKE: Several cupcakes, laid out side by side, iced together to look like one big cake. Allows you to serve an assortment of cake flavors—a godsend when dealing with a passel of picky eaters.

CAKE POPS: Cake on a stick! Some look like minicupcakes, others (usually professionally made) are little balls of cake more closely resembling lollipops. Fun for kids and adults and cuts down on sticky, messy hands afterward.

 THREE DAYS BEFORE

Buy ingredients, if making menu yourself.

Confirm entertainment and any other hired help.

Assemble goodie bags.

 ONE TO TWO DAYS BEFORE

Charge camera, cell phone, video camera, and so on.

Bake or pick up cake and/or cupcakes.

Confirm party duties with all enlisted friends and family.

 DAY OF PARTY

Have delivery menu from local pizzeria on hand, just in case of any food emergencies.

Decorate! Leave yourself a couple hours for this.

Take "before" photo of party area.

Enjoy! You did it!

 THE WEEK AFTER

Send party photos and videos to parents, family members–especially those who couldn't attend.

## From Goodie to Great!

## Party Planning Through the Ages

Using the outline I just gave you for throwing a one-year-old's party, you'll only need to make a few easy adjustments to tailor that template to any age.

AGES TWO AND UP: Give kids a say on the guest list. A good general rule is that once a niece or nephew is old enough to remember a friend by name, you can start inviting that friend to parties.

AGES THREE AND UP: Check with your niece or nephew as well as parents on theme ideas they like. (To frame the discussion productively, ask questions like, "Do you want a princess birthday or a Dora birthday? Do you want a pink birthday or a purple birthday? What is your favorite book? What is your favorite video?")

Start incorporating games with simple rules into the party, like Simon Says or Pin the Tail on the Donkey. (As long as it's hung low enough, a piñata can work for kids this age, too!)

# Family Matters

I know that family events don't always go smoothly. Got relatives who don't get along? Tips for keeping the peace:

❋ Host the party at a large public venue, like a park or a community center's multipurpose room, so everyone can maintain some space (and not find things around the house to criticize!).

❋ Note on the invitation an exact beginning and end to the party.

❋ Give warring family members party-helping duties that keep them out of each other's hair.

❋ Call those you think will have issue with another guest and try to curtail any problems in advance.

❋ Once the cake is cut, people are on their own if they can't figure out how to get into a good mood.

AGES FOUR AND UP: Now's when the guest list will really start to swell with friends (from preschool, T-ball, etc.) more than family, so cross-check any menu planning with kids' parents in case of allergies. (Peanut butter cookies? Don't even go there.)

AGES FIVE AND UP: Party games can start getting more complex. Try sack races, three-legged races, Twister, or a scavenger hunt. The kids are old enough now to send thank-you notes for birthday gifts received–but still, a dozen or so thank-you notes may be a lot for a child of this age. Try buying a pack of thank-you notes and asking your niece or nephew to just do a quick drawing on the inside. Or mail a recent fingerpainting project as a thank-you. (Older relatives will especially appreciate this!)

# Holidays!

What's a holiday without the most precious people in your life to share it with? And for the kids, having their auntie on hand (or even on the phone or Skype, when she's a Long-Distance Auntie) is a big reason why these occasions are so special. In fact, with the parents so often extrabusy during the holiday season—wrapping, cooking, decorating, shopping—an auntie can actually help just by making herself available to her nieces and nephews. And once you've got that time with them, I've got all kinds of ways to create and commemorate family traditions.

## Seven Ways a Savvy Auntie Can Make Every Holiday Special

1. Talk to your nieces and nephews in the days and weeks beforehand about what age- and holiday-appropriate auntivities they want to share with you, whether it's baking cookies, making their own holiday cards, sewing a costume, playing with a dreidel, or dyeing Easter eggs.

2. Share stories with them of years past. Dust off old photo albums and show them pictures of you and your siblings from your younger years–they'll get such a kick out of seeing their parents as children! Likewise, include stories about their first few years of life–they will love hearing about themselves!

3. Give presents that will last a lifetime. Little nieces might love a charm bracelet that they can add onto in the years to come, or a dollhouse that can be augmented with new furnishings in the future. For nephews, try starting off with a few baseball cards from his favorite team and an album to hold them in, then add to the collection every year.

4. Offer to take your nieces and nephews shopping so they can select gifts for their parents. This gets you more quality time with them–and gives Mom and Dad time to wrap gifts in secret! (Or just have a drink, if that's what they need.)

5. With Mom and Dad's permission, take older nieces and nephews to volunteer at a local charity. It'll remind them that the holidays aren't just about getting presents, and it may be the start of a whole new auntie tradition.

6. Long-Distance Aunties who can't make it out to see the nieces and nephews can send more than presents. Kids will love care packages with baked goods and sweets. Include the recipes you used, and a note promising to make them with the kids the next time you visit.

7. **Get outdoors!** Too often, holidays mean being trapped in the house. Find something seasonal to do, like ice skating, a haunted house, a holiday market, or an Easter egg hunt. It'll give the kids a chance to burn off some of that holiday energy!

## Believing in Santa Claus and Other Holiday Icons

Inevitably, a niece or nephew will one day ask: Is there such a thing as Santa Claus? Or, if you dodge that one, you might wind up getting grilled about the Easter Bunny, the Tooth Fairy, the Great Pumpkin, and so on. This is one doozy of a question that no parent or Savvy Auntie wants to field. But I happen to know a pair of fail-safe replies that'll work for kids of all ages:

1. **"What do you think?"**

2. **"Anything you believe is true to you."**

# First Day of School!

The first day of school is probably the biggest event in a young niece's or nephew's life, which can be both awfully exciting and fraught with fear. Luckily, Mom, Dad, and Auntie are there to offer encouragement and support, and to make the adventure one filled with fun and discovery.

For starters, there's school shopping to do! Supplies, outfits, shoes, a backpack, and a lunch box are necessities. Although shopping sprees are often Savvy Auntie's specialty, hold on. Mom may be eager to take on this memorable task herself, especially if it's her firstborn. A few kids down the road, though, Mom and Dad might be thrilled for you to take a turn with this to-do.

If you do get the go-ahead, by all means invite your niece or nephew to come shopping with you. Even five-year-olds have discerning tastes these days. And whether you shop alone or with the kids, get a list of their favorite cartoon characters, who can accompany them to school splashed across an eco-friendly water bottle or notebook cover.

For preschoolers and kindergartners, school supplies are often more about letting them feel like big kids, so get them what will encourage them to feel good about learning. If your niece wants a princess pencil case, for example, go ahead. Of course, I recommend you check out discount retailers, overstock stores, and dollar stores for these kinds of supplies, especially since some items may get misplaced before school even starts.

## *Auntie Up!* **What Are Your Favorite Holiday Traditions?**

I have two six-year-old grandnieces who live across the country and who I've only met in person once before. I've been sending them their own Christmas cards since they were two. Then, just last week, I saw them at a family reunion. At first, they didn't remember me at all—but then their mother told them I was "the Christmas card aunt" and I was in like Flynn!

—Tina Holcomb, South Orange, NJ

As I got more and more involved with running and triathlons, I wanted to share my healthy lifestyle with my family. I decided to start Shigo Family Fun Day. It's celebrated at every holiday we're together, usually Thanksgiving, Christmas, and Easter. The sharing of a physical activity together was the goal. The first year, I put water bottles in everyone's Christmas stockings with a small note declaring the first Shigo Family Fun Day. We all headed out on bikes and although it didn't last long, we all had fun. We hiked one year, which was wonderful. Last year, our celebration was an excursion to the bowling alley.

—Amy Shigo, New York, NY

My nephew and I keep my mom's memory alive by making angel ornaments every year. He always reminds me in October to buy the stuff for it!

—Samantha Tuman, Chicago, IL

I buy them each an ornament, so that once they are old enough to have their own tree, they will have enough eclectic ornaments to make them feel like they are "home for the holidays" wherever they may roam.

—Mary L. Cottingham, Belle Mead, NJ

*The holiday tradition I started with my nieces is to decorate our front door like a present. They know what Tiffany & Co. is, thanks to me, so we made our door a Tiffany box last year.*

—Marlene Ramirez, Alhambra, CA

*For nearly ten years my nephew and I went to the Cincinnati Zoo's Festival of Lights. We started when he was five and he thinks the last time we went he was thirteen. Our tradition within the tradition was to get warm cinnamon almonds from a vendor there. I do know that the last time we went, all we cared about were the almonds! Great memories!*

—Sue Remmy, Cincinnati, OH

*Do you know a book called Auntie Claus? Well, my nephews do—because we read it every Christmas. Then we go to church for evening service and they come home to a present on their beds from Auntie Claus—brand-new handmade pajamas. They know it's me, but they can't wait to see what I've done. (Bonus! Christmas morning they have new pajamas on in all the pictures!)*

—Jamie Fiorino, Spokane, WA

# Special Occasion Snaptitude!

For all the planning you put into sharing special time with your nieces and nephews, you're going to want to take top-notch photos that'll capture the memories in a marvelous fashion. Heed this expert advice from New York City photographer Heidi Green, renowned for her party pics of Gotham's kiderati.

📷 **SCHEDULE YOUR SHOTS.**

Always get a party's agenda beforehand so you're prepared to take all the right photos at the right time. Things not to miss: presents being opened, candles being blown out, a niece or nephew laying eyes on Santa (a Savvy Uncle in disguise!) for the very first time.

📷 **YOUR CAMERA SHOULD BE A CAMERA.**

Your smartphone may be fabulous (and some do take amazing photos), but you don't want a text buzzing in just as the perfect pose presents itself. Digital cameras are becoming more and more affordable and really are the way to go. Because kids don't sit still, look for cameras designed for spontaneous shots, that handle movement well, and that require minimal time between snaps.

📷 **GET DOWN!**

Pics taken from a tot's-eye view will be imbued with wonder-filled perspective, so crouch down to the ground. (And maybe don't wear a skirt.)

📷 **INCLUDE COSTARS.**

Don't forget the siblings, parents, grandparents, pets, a favorite doll or stuffed animal, or a b-day boy's or girl's young friends. That cute pigtailed girl your nephew gave his cupcake to might grow up to be his prom date, after all.

## *The most magical moments are rarely those that were planned . . .*

📷 **DON'T FLASH THE KIDS.**

(Not that kind of flashing, Auntie!) Use natural light to illuminate your subjects instead of the camera's built-in flash; it frightens some kids, and like anyone, it can have them seeing spots.

📷 **DON'T FORGET THE DECORATIONS.**

Professional photogs often call these detail shots: piles of presents, hanging decor, a stylishly set table, and especially any cake or cupcakes baked with care by Mom. (In fact, shoot those from a number of angles, and take a close-up of birthday candles.)

📷 **SURPRISE!**

The most magical moments are rarely those that were planned and posed by a grown-up. So take lots of candid shots and keep your eyes open for the unexpected.

📷 **HAVE FUN!**

I know, Auntie: The pressure! The stress! Don't worry, you'll do great. Have fun and it will all come naturally. And if not, there are always Grandpa's pics to fall back on.

(By the way, before you go shopping, ask Mom or Dad if your niece's or nephew's school sent home a list of the school supplies she or he will need. Depending on the grade and the teacher, this can vary widely from year to year or from child to child. Sometimes it's a lot less or a lot more than you might think.)

## School Books

To calm first-day jitters, talk to the kids about what to expect, remind them which of their little friends will now be their classmates, and tell them a story about your first day of school. Or do what aunties do best—read them a book! Karen Gallagher, founder of the Lollipop Book Club, a children's book-of-the-month club, suggests these five fail-safe books to help young children acclimate to their first day of school:

*My First Day at Nursery School*
    By Becky Edwards
    Illustrated by Anthony Flintoft
    Ages 2–4

*Countdown to Kindergarten*
    By Allison McGhee
    Illustrated by Harry Bliss
    Ages 4–6

*The Kissing Hand*
    By Audrey Penn
    Ages 4–8

*First Day Jitters*
    By Julie Danneberg
    Illustrated by Judith Dufour Love
    Ages 4–8

*First Grade Stinks*
    By Mary Ann Rodman
    Illustrated by Beth Spiegel
    Ages 5–7

# Gift-Giving Savvy: Fauntastic Toys, Clothes, and Books

IF A SAVVY AUNTIE IS known for one thing, it's being a fabulous gift giver. We load the kids up with as much joy as we can, and it's not hard to see why most of us *love indulging our nieces and nephews* with the hottest toys and games—because it makes them so happy! Which, frankly, makes us happy, too. Plus, we get to maintain our savvy status with each "It's so cool! It's just what I wanted!"

However, even the Savviest Auntie might not necessarily know exactly what her nieces and nephews want (or what their parents approve or disapprove of). The littlest kids are too tiny to say, while the bigger ones are fans of shows and movies (with tie-in merchandise) we've never heard of. And unlike parents, we're not hearing earloads of wish lists during the daily carpool or around the nightly dinner table.

We also may have lost some perspective on the age appropriateness of certain gifts. (Hey, it's been a while since we've been kids ourselves!) Of course we know that boys may prefer trucks while girls go for dolls, but which trucks are best for what age? Would a five-year-old niece want a baby doll or a fashion doll? When do kids start wearing shoes? When do they start to read to themselves?

Never fear, Auntie dear! This chapter tells you everything you need to know about picking out the perfect toys, clothes, and books. After all, that's just what us Savvy Aunties do.

# Choose the Right Toys

Most toys come with appropriate ages clearly marked, so take heed, Auntie! Those recommendations are there for good reason. No matter how advanced you believe your niece or nephew is, a four-year-old will become frustrated by a toy she or he lacks the fine motor skills to operate. Seven-year-olds, on the other hand, often become bored with toys designed for younger kids. Even an age difference of only a few months can matter. A four-month-old, for example, can't hold on to a toy that has already lost the interest of an eighteen-month-old sibling.

Remember that as much as we want to believe that specially designed learning toys will help our nieces and nephews develop, what is much more critical is our playtime interactions with them. Auntie and child playing with a toy together is infinitely more worthwhile than giving a child a "smart" toy and then heading out the door.

Since some toys are hot today and then left cold on the basement floor tomorrow, the following list focuses on age-appropriate types of toys, not specific brand names:

### 0 to 6 months

Activity gyms or mats

Teething accessories

Large interlocking rings or keys

Musical and chiming toys

Rattles

### 6 to 12 months

Nesting cups, stacking rings, etc.

Pop-up toys

Soft blocks

Bath toys

Squeeze/squeak toys

### 1 to 2 Years

Foot-propelled, ride-on toys

Wagons

Play household items (telephone, lawn mower, workbench, shopping cart, etc.)

Sandbox and wading pool toys

Nontoxic art supplies (crayons and coloring books, clay, finger paints, etc.)

### 2 to 3 Years

Building blocks, hard-sided blocks with letters and numbers

Dolls that can be bathed, fed, and diapered

Hand/finger puppets

Play scenes (farm, airport) with figures and accessories

Tricycle and helmet

# Auntie Up! What's the Best Gift You Ever Got 'Em?

Looking for a present they'll remember far into the future? Some real-life Savvy Aunties hit the jackpot with these generous goodies!

*An iPod when she was five, a swing set when she was six, thousands of dollars spent at Build-a-Bear. . . . This is why I park my car in the garage, so if the repo man drives down my street, he won't see it and keep driving!*

—Kristin Love Webseter, Monee, IL

*A Power Wheels for my nephew when he turned two. A DSi for my niece when she turned five.*

—Elizabeth Dawn Dishon, Baltimore, MD

*The diamond from my promise ring. I had it reset into a necklace for her to wear to her first semiformal dance. I felt even better about it than when I received it for a gift.*

—Pauline Parker Brannigan, New Milford, CT

*Each year I take my nieces back-to-school shopping and get them all the new clothes they need for fall.*

—Beth Bonina, Brooklyn, NY

*I recently let my nephew help me pick out a brand-new car with the intention of passing it on to him once he's old enough to drive it. He was so excited that he was included in making the decision—and that he will inherit a pretty cool car!*

—Melissa Mello, Fresno, CA

### 3 to 6 Years

10- to 20-piece puzzles

Dolls that can be dressed and undressed

Props for make-believe play (costumes, play tools, play makeup kit, etc.)

Music/CD player

Simple board games (involving counting, matching, memory skills, etc.)

### 6 to 9 Years

Sporting equipment (baseball glove, hockey stick, tennis racket) with protective gear

Action figures

Fashion/career dolls

Model, craft, science, or magic kits

Jigsaw/3-D puzzles

### 9 to 12 Years

Advanced construction sets

Remote-controlled vehicles

Playing cards

Chess, checkers, dominoes, strategy games

Recreational weaponry (light sabers, Super Soakers, etc.)

Source: Toy Industry Association

## Anything You Can Play, I Can Play Better . . .

Determined to make sure your nieces and nephews grow up to be whomever they want to be, you might be tempted to staunchly stick to gender-neutral toys for your tots, or even considering a gender-bending present, like a truck for a girl or a baking set for a boy.

I hear you, but I've also seen the research on this, so I just want to warn you that your niece may use the flatbed of her new truck as a crib for her dollies, while a little boy's baking set may become an action-figure oven. Numerous studies have shown that babies start exhibiting "typical" male and female behaviors as soon as three hours after being born—well before society can have its way with their impressionable young minds.

Quite simply, little boys and girls are fascinated by different things. (In a nutshell, baby girls are into human motions and sounds. Boys get jazzed by mechanical motions and sounds.) Also, certain cognitive and motor skills develop faster in boys than girls, and vice versa, which means a toy that one of them finds enthralling, the other might not possess the capacity to enjoy yet.

Still not convinced? Here's a quick roundup of what numerous studies have concluded about the battle of the baby sexes.

*Quite simply, little boys and girls are fascinated by different things.*

GIRLS . . .

❋ start talking before boys do.

❋ respond better to human voices than mechanical sounds like a shaken rattle.

❋ are better at maintaining eye contact.

❋ excel at imitating expressions, such as sticking out their tongues, only hours after being born.

❋ as toddlers, excel at copying behaviors they've witnessed, such as taking care of a baby!

BOYS . . .

❋ prefer observing mechanical motion (windshield wipers, a spinning mobile) over human emotion (expressions, etc.).

❋ prefer looking at a group of many faces rather than one individual face.

❋ develop much stronger gross motor skills (walking, kicking, ball throwing) by the time they reach preschool age.

❋ express fear less often.

# Savvy Safety: Toy Tips

We all want to give our nieces and nephews toys that will make them smile. But more important, we want those toys to be safe. Here are eight ways a Savvy Auntie can help to ensure fun and safe toy play.

1. Carefully read a toy's packaging and labels for safety warnings and recommended age ranges—which are based on a toy's potential safety hazards, not on how smart a child may be.

2. Especially for kids three and under, sturdy parts and tightly secured joints are a must. Avoid any toy with sharp edges, toxic materials, and small pieces that might separate or be broken off.

3. Once the thrill of gift opening is done, remove all that used gift wrap and plastic packaging as soon as possible. Piles of wrapping paper can conceal sharp objects, and the edges of hard plastic packaging can cut small fingers.

4. Always read assembly and usage instructions. Encourage the parents to hang on to product literature in case of future questions. Filling out and mailing back warranty cards is essential so that parents can be contacted in case of a toy recall.

5. For safe toy storage, parents should keep a separate toy chest or bin for older children's toys, which may contain small parts. Make sure these older kids know it's also their responsibility to help keep their toys out of the reach of younger siblings. Lidded toy storage should be nonlocking and have special safety features such as spring-loaded hinges to make sure little fingers won't get caught.

6. Did you know that more toy-related "boo-boos" are caused by trips and falls than by toys themselves? Keep staircases and high-traffic hallways toy-free!

7. Always supervise a young child's playtime.

8. Inspect toys regularly. Repair or replace damaged or broken parts immediately.

Source: www.Toyinfo.org

# Kiddie Couture

Kids' and babies' outfits are so darn adorable, we Savvy Aunties can't help ourselves. We'll take the entire store, PANK you very much!

Before you go crazy on cute couture, read up on how to give garments that fit and function properly.

## Sizing

Most important, of course, is buying the right size. Which is not easy: Stores sometimes mark clothes differently from one another, as do European versus American manufacturers. Always double-check with an employee or the store's sizing chart online.

### BABY

Clothes are sized by month, based on the average weight and length of a baby at that age. (Preemies, of course, may be smaller than average. It's often difficult to find stuff for them, but you can look for special items labeled "up to 7 pounds" and "up to 17 inches.")

Baby sizes go up to 24 months of age and are made to fit up to that month, not beyond.

**0-3 months: 7 to 12 lbs, 17 to 23 inches (sometimes just called "newborn")**

**3-6 months: 12 to 17 lbs, 23 to 27 inches**

**6-12 months: 17 to 22 lbs, 27 to 29 inches**

**12-18 months: 22 to 27 lbs, 29 to 31 inches**

**18-24 months: 27 to 30 lbs, 31 to 33 inches**

### TODDLER

Sizes are often marked by a "T" and go by year. 2T, for example, is for two-year-olds (which some stores may still call "24 months and up"). Sizing goes up to 5T. Some stores start three-year-olds in the "big kids" department with a size 4. . . . Yes, this is when it gets complicated.

## BIG KIDS

Sometimes sized numerically, sometimes by XS, S, M, L, XL and XXL. Or sometimes they stop at L. Sometimes divided into boy and girl sizes. And some brands make plus/hefty and/or slim sizes. Definitely read the tags and consult sizing charts.

**3- to 4-year-olds: Size 4 or XS**

**4- to 5-year-olds: Size 5 or S**

**5- to 6-year-olds: Size 6 or S**

**6- to 7-year-olds: Size 6X/7 or M**

**7- to 8-year-olds: Size 8 or M**

**8- to 9-year-olds: Size 10 or L**

**9- to 10-year-olds: Size 12 or XXL**

**10+-year-olds: Size 14 or XXL**

## SHOES AND SOCKS

No matter how cute the shoes, babies do not need them until they start walking. In fact, shoes may impede proper foot development if worn too soon. Some shoes that are soft and pliable are OK for colder months, or as the baby starts to stand on her feet from a crawling position. Of course, once that baby does start walking (soon after his or her first birthday, usually), stylish, comfortable footwear is a necessity.

Again, there is no universal sizing for shoes, and they can be really hard to size correctly without the child present. If you want to attempt a shoe purchase, ask a parent for a specific size from a specific shoe store, and get a gift receipt!

Socks are often sized by age, which is noted on the label.

# Book 'Em, Auntie

Every now and then you see a movie or TV show where a reluctant adult tries to get away with "reading" the sports pages or reciting stock quotes to a baby. Funny, but not ideal.

Different kinds of books allow kids to make use of the cognitive abilities they have at a certain stage in life before progressing onward and upward to more intricately drawn illustrations, bigger words, and more complicated plots. While at first you'll be reading aloud to your nieces and nephews, before you know it, they will want to "read" along with you (pointing at pages that interest them, adding their own commentary, asking you to skip ahead or go back, etc.). Soon they'll graduate to reading on their own!

## Newborns to One Year

### SOFT BOOKS

Cloth or plastic books, usually wordless, that can be read to a baby from day one. Some double as teething toys or rattles with their crinkly sounds and textures. Plastic ones are perfect for bath time!

### WORDLESS BOOKS

Add your own words to the pictures when "reading" the book to a baby.

### NURSERY RHYMES

Classic nursery rhyme books are always beloved.

## Toddlers Ages One to Three

### BOARD BOOKS

Hard textured, made from cardboard instead of paper. Withstand a lot of wear and tear, which is good since small children like their favorites read to them again and again. They also like to put their mouths on them and chew from time to time.

### EARLY PICTURE BOOKS

Typically no more than three hundred words long, focusing on color, shapes, letters, and numbers. Some include textures, pop-ups, or flaps to make the experience more interactive.

# Buyer Beware! Suggestions on Becoming Your Niece's or Nephew's Personal Shopper

It's always your prerogative to buy whatever you want for your niece or nephew. A cashmere sweater she'll outgrow in three months? Sure! Wool trousers for a nephew too young to walk? Why not? A holiday dress she'll wear once? Of course! However, by taking some more practical considerations into account, you'll up your chances that they'll don your designer duds more frequently and adorably. (Which, P.S., is largely determined by how much the parents approve of your picks.)

Remember these caveats next time you go on a cute-fueled shopping spree:

* Dry-clean-only garments will not be a parent's favorite. Babies are notorious for spitting up, and toddlers love nothing more than spilling juice and melted ice cream.

* Mom's approval is especially important for coats and special-occasion wear. A coat is something she's got to get on their bodies every day, while a party outfit will likely be remembered in photos forever. So Mom is going to want to love both.

* Itchy clothing is a no-no. You don't like wearing scratchy slacks, and neither does your nephew. Not even for a minute. Not even just for one photo.

* Before buying a onesie, see how quickly you can snap and unsnap, button and unbutton it. A complicated one's not going to survive long in the clothing rotation.

  I discovered a new type of onesie from a company called Magnificent Baby, cofounded by a Savvy Auntie who felt that changing her baby nephew—with all those snaps, and the Velcro that got caught in his hair—was harder than it needed to be. Her savvy solution: Magnets for closures! Makes changing a snap—without the snaps!

When shopping for same-sex twins, try buying complementary, instead of identical, outfits. Get the same sundress in two different colors, or buy the same cargo shorts but with different T-shirts to match.

Honestly, if Mom and Dad love something you bought before, just buy more of that. Frequent the stores they frequent and stick to the brands they're loyal to.

Once kids are old enough to speak up about what they like—usually the age they start throwing fits about what they don't want to put on—go for outfits in their favorite colors, or T-shirts with their favorite characters on them. Auntie just helped to avoid a meltdown!

And just in case, shop stores that are close to Mom and Dad and have generous, flexible return policies. If exchanging an item becomes a hassle, it'll probably be forever relegated to the bottom of the drawer.

## Ages Four to Eight

### EARLY READERS

Usually a board book with less than a thousand words, perfect for a beginner transitioning from toddler books.

### PICTURE BOOKS

Classically, these are thirty-two pages long (about fifteen hundred words) and take the point of view of one lead character. They're meant to be read to the child first, then read independently.

## Ages Six to Nine

### EARLY CHAPTER BOOKS

Read like a picture book but look more like a chapter book—just like the one an older sibling may be reading. Either thirty-two or sixty-four pages long.

## Ages Seven to Ten

### CHAPTER BOOKS

Hardcover or paperback books that look more like adult novels for the junior set. Chapters are short (about three or four pages); the entire book may be forty-five to sixty pages in length.

## Board-Book Authors and Illustrators Every Savvy Auntie Should Know

Byron Barton: *Planes; Trucks; Boats; Machines at Work; My Car.*
   Filled with bold colors, symmetrical shapes, and all kinds of vehicles boys love.

Sandra Boynton: *Barnyard Dance!; Oh My, Oh My, Oh Dinosaurs!; One, Two, Three!; Pajama Time!; Hey! Wake Up!; Birthday Monsters!*
   Quirky animals engaging in silly behavior teach little children colors, numbers, and other fundamentals in a thoroughly fun way.

Margaret Wise Brown: *Goodnight Moon; The Runaway Bunny; Big Red Barn.*
   A prolific writer of numerous classics; a niece or nephew is sure to love several.

# Reading Is (Fun!)damental

To integrate reading into auntiehood:

Read everywhere! Read store signs, flyers on the refrigerator, birthday cards. Words are everywhere, waiting to be learned.

If you're looking for an activity centered around reading, take them to the library or local bookstore for storytelling events.

Don't have a book? Make up a story or tell them a fairy tale you remember as a child—putting them in the middle of it by using their names for the characters. (Try writing one down sometime when you've got a free hand. Savvy Crafty Auntie can then gift the tale back to her niece or nephew in the form of a little handmade book!)

Long-Distance Aunties: once your niece or nephew is old enough to manipulate the pages of a book without assistance, use Skype, a smartphone, or other videoconferencing technology to read her or him a story even when you're not there. Turn it into a little book-of-the-month club by mailing the child a personal copy of the book beforehand (kids love getting their own mail!).

Eric Carle: *The Very Hungry Caterpillar; The Very Quiet Cricket; The Very Busy Spider; From Head to Toe; Brown Bear, Brown Bear, What Do You See?* (written by Bill Martin Jr., illustrated by Eric Carle); *Polar Bear, Polar Bear, What Do You Hear?* (written by Bill Martin Jr., illustrated by Eric Carle).
 Noted for his distinctive collage art and creative page formatting.

Karen Katz: *Where Is Baby's Belly Button?; What Does Baby Say?; Where Is Baby's Mommy?*
 Known for her colorful, interactive, lift-the-flap books, enormously popular with toddlers.

# Picture-Book Authors Every Savvy Auntie Should Know

**Ian Falconer:** The *Olivia* series; *Dream Big.*

Rarely has a picture-book author experienced as much success with a single character as Falconer has. His sassy swine, Olivia, is an endearing pig with a penchant for getting into mischief.

**Kevin Henkes:** *Olive's Ocean; Lilly's Purple Plastic Purse; Chrysanthemum; Sheila Rae; Kitten's First Full Moon.*

Many of Henkes's stories are packed with valuable lessons, based on his real-life childhood growing up in Racine, Wisconsin, and feature strong-willed female characters.

**Laura Numeroff:** *If You Give a Pig a Pancake; If You Give a Mouse a Cookie; If You Take a Mouse to the Movies; If You Give a Moose a Muffin.*

Numeroff's books often are based on "what if?" scenarios that pique the interest of toddlers and encourage them to think about cause and effect through the experiences of friendly, albeit pesky, little animals.

**Shel Silverstein:** *Where the Sidewalk Ends; The Giving Tree; A Light in the Attic; Falling Up; The Missing Piece.*

The king of kids' kooky poetry, a crafter of thought-provoking prose, and a penciller of whimsical doodles.

**Chris Van Allsburg:** *The Polar Express; Jumanji; The Garden of Abdul Gasazi; Just a Dream; Two Bad Ants; Zathura.*

Van Allsburg has written and illustrated a plethora of books with captivating story lines and illustrations. His pictures are drawn from the perspective and height of a child, capturing the world on paper in the way only an accomplished artist can.

**Mo Willems:** *Don't Let the Pigeon Drive the Bus!; Knuffle Bunny; Leonardo the Terrible Monster.*

Kids laugh at the anthropomorphic facial expressions and are especially captivated by the cartoon-on-photo artwork displayed.

**Jane Yolen:** *Owl Moon; Mama's Kiss; Briar Rose;* the *How Do Dinosaurs?* series.

The *New York Times* has called Yolen "a modern equivalent of Aesop," while *Newsweek* claims she's the "Hans Christian Andersen of America."

## Chapter-Book Authors Every Savvy Auntie Should Know

**Judy Blume:** *Tales of a Fourth Grade Nothing; Blubber; Superfudge; Otherwise Known as Sheila the Great; Freckle Juice.*

Many Savvy Aunties will remember reading Blume's young-adult classics, but she also wrote several chapter books that are perfectly suited for grade-schoolers.

**Andrew Clements:** *Frindle; Extra Credit; No Talking; A Week in the Woods; Lunch Money; The Landry News.*

Writes primarily about schooltime adventures. His children's novels are entertaining, quick reads that keep kids coming back for more.

**Roald Dahl:** *Charlie and the Chocolate Factory; James and the Giant Peach; Fantastic Mr. Fox; Matilda.*

Dahl's dark humor and twisted perspective pervade his captivating, if unsentimental and occasionally violent, prose.

**E. L. Konigsburg:** *From the Mixed-up Files of Mrs. Basil E. Frankweiler; The View from Saturday; The Outcasts of 19 Schuyler Place.*

Konigsburg's novels tackle adolescent struggles and often concern a child's quest to shape his or her identity–wrapped up in a quirky adventure.

**Lois Lowry:** *The Giver; Messenger; Gathering Blue; Number the Stars; Gooney Bird Greene; A Summer to Die.*

Tackles complex issues in children's books for more advanced readers: racism, the Holocaust, terminal illness, and murder. Her writing has provoked controversy, so check with Mom and Dad before buying her books.

**Louis Sachar:** *Holes; Small Steps; Sideways Stories from Wayside School; There's a Boy in the Girls' Bathroom; Kidnapped at Birth?*

His successful series books as well as individual novels have been read by kids for more than thirty years.

## Anything You Can Read, I Can Read Better . . .

I know there are plenty of books that girls love just as much as boys. For whatever reason, the opposite usually doesn't apply; not too many boys sit down with a copy of *Fancy Nancy* or *Pinkalicious.* (Although if they do, that's great. Reading is reading!)

# Spoiling

Giving gifts does come with a challenge. Though we want to please and provide, we don't want to spoil. When does gift giving cross the line into spoiling? If you think of spoiling as giving things in lieu of love, then it's easy to figure out how not to spoil. Give love first, but supplement with gifts. Otherwise, your niece or nephew will indicate her or his spoiled attitude by acting blasé, as if your presents are not special.

## *Auntie Up!* How Do You Know When It's Spoiling?

**Spoiling is one of those things you can't define, but you know it when you see it. Take heed if one of the following niece- or nephew-spoiling scenarios happen to you.**

*You know it's officially spoiling when they prefer to live with you and not the parents! Mom is not as "cool" as Auntie!*

—Farrah Pullin, Atlanta, GA

*It's officially spoiling them when you buy them two limited-edition bags and one throws hers on the floor and says, "I wanted Keroppi, not Hello Kitty!" Also when one of them tells a classmate, "This is Baby Phat. See my tag? My auntie taught me how to spot fakes." I was mortified!*

—Marlene Ramirez, Alhambra, CA

*I think it is officially called "spoiling" when Mom and Dad say no and they know Aunt Dawni will say yes!*

—Elizabeth Dawn Dishon, Baltimore, MD

# A Is for Auntie

7

# The Importance of Qualauntie Time

"AUNTIE TIME IS QUALITY TIME." That's a quote from my conversation with Dr. Rose-

marie Truglio, vice president of research and education at Sesame Workshop. She went on to say,

"An aunt is not a teacher. *An aunt is all about quality time*–and really, time to play."

This means that all the ways that we aunties interact with our young nieces and nephews–

playing alongside them, reading them the same book three times in a row just because they want

to hear it again and again, making up new games–can be critical to their cognitive, social, and

# Kids Getting Older Younger

There's a trend called "Kids Getting Older Younger," a.k.a. KGOY, which refers to the way young children are influenced today. Toys that we played with when we were four or five are now being taken up by toddlers. And once they get to school, they learn in first grade what you and I learned in second—what the authors of *Einstein Never Used Flash Cards* call a "new kind of 'grade inflation.'" There's a race to educate children faster and sooner than ever before. And it's putting pressure on kids who really just want to play.

emotional development and future academic successes. In fact, you, dear Auntie, may be one of the few adults in your niece's or nephew's life who can provide that playful early education. (Quite jaw-dropping to realize, no?)

These days, there's a lot of pressure on parents to make sure their children are budding into baby geniuses with every passing day. After all, tykes sometimes have to take standardized tests just to get accepted into a good preschool! Meanwhile, with Mom and Dad doing double duty handling their careers and the household, the notion of carving out quality playtime often remains an elusive luxury. This is where qualauntie time comes in, because children learn best just by doing what they do best: play.

Play. As Kathy Hirsh-Pasek and Roberta Michnick Golinkoff state in their book *Einstein Never Used Flash Cards,* play has become a four-letter word. It's as if letting children just play is a waste of time, when really it's an opportunity for them to discover things—learn things—through having fun. At play, they create their own games and use their imaginations. Not only does this develop cognition, it also gives kids a sense of mastery and independence, the authors say, which is what they need to enjoy managing their own lives.

Need more proof? Zero to Three, a nonprofit organization that fosters early childhood education, agrees that play appears to lay the developmental groundwork in babies and toddlers for better literacy down the road. Pretending—building imaginary worlds, creating symbols to represent other things—is like an early form of reading and writing. The group recommends a daily hour of unstructured play for a young child.

This is why your role is so important, Auntie. When we visit with our nieces and nephews, it's about tea parties, role playing, and make-believe. It's about play.

(If your niece's or nephew's parents ask you to help them with something like flash-card memorization, I support your doing so. However, that doesn't mean that afterward, you can't head outside to play in the mud. Unless you're wearing white pants. But that's entirely up to you, Auntie.)

In fact, it takes very little effort to help a niece or nephew this way. All you need is this one simple guideline: be a positive auntie. Give your nieces and nephews time to play, give them love, offer guidance and support, and respond to their needs.

And just in case you need a few more guidelines, the following are some expert-recommended suggestions for fun, educational, innovative, and interactive "qualauntie time."

## Baby Talk

Whenever you're with your little niece or nephew, even before she or he is old enough to talk back, you should talk, talk, talk! This may sound simple, but even when it's just an auntie and a child, there can be distractions: an incoming text, a morning-news headline, a whistling teakettle. The trick is to always keep your one-way conversation going.

When you go for a walk together, describe what you see around you. Talk about what the child is wearing. Talk about your surroundings. Studies have shown that children of low-income families have a vocabulary deficit that results from not being spoken to enough as babies. These children begin school at a deficit, too, often never catching up. So keep talking.

Once your niece or nephew is old enough to start saying some basic words—even if it's "moo" for milk or "duh" for dog—open up the discussion and keep it going. Rather than just getting the milk when you hear "moo," say, "You want some milk, sweetie? Auntie will get you some nice milk." And then: "Here is your milk, sweetie." And: "Sweetie is drinking milk. Milk is yummy."

Although replicating a niece's or nephew's goo-goo talk isn't productive, talking in a babyish pitch is. In fact, small children better understand higher-pitched, singsong voices. It's their cue that we're talking to them, and it heightens their attention to what we're saying and the words we're using. When we speak in this "infant-directed speech," or IDS—which again, is different from babbling like a baby—our vowels are longer and easier for them to understand. We also tend to speak more slowly, enabling babies to make out separate words. (It's even been shown that adults better learn a foreign language when they're taught it in IDS!)

Once your niece or nephew is speaking in full sentences, here's a little wordplay game I recommend. Instead of telling a niece or nephew, "I love you," say something like, "I love you as high as the sky!" Or "I love you as big as the sun!" While this is a beautiful way to share your love, it's also a very good education in spatial relations. As proof, a little boy I know decided to have fun with it one day and stated, "I love you teeny tiny little itsy bitsy like an ant!" And so I replied, "I still love you as big as the sun!" To which he said, "I love you teeny tiny itsy bitsy like the little tiny bitsy ant's eye," squeezing his forefinger and thumb tightly together to represent this idea. And so on. He got smaller and smaller and I got bigger and bigger. (And yes, he did later admit to loving me as big as the universe before it ended.)

Use singing and rhyming, too. Singing the same song to a child can improve memory and vocabulary. Reciting familiar children's poems and nursery rhymes also helps. Why not create your own rhyme or song? If your niece or nephew has a favorite pet, doll, or stuffed animal, make up a song about it. Even better, write a song about a food she or he doesn't like as a way to encourage her or him to try it again. Remember the song, because you'll be fielding requests for it again and again!

## Get Your Motor Runnin'

For most kids, motor skills are first developed through stacking, building, and connecting all sorts of rings, blocks, LEGOs, and so on. Connecting train tracks or race-car tracks also helps develop motor skills and coordination, as well as providing a strong sense of spatial relations and physics. (What goes up the track must come down the track!)

And don't forget music! Play a happy tune and a baby who's only a few months old will wiggle around to the beat. Dancing helps improve a child's coordination, balance, and rhythm. Best of all, playing an instrument, like a baby xylophone, is great for motor skills and sensory development.

Dr. Rosmarie Truglio suggested these activities to seamlessly turn playful time into learning time:

❋ **Puzzles:** Puzzles are great for hand-eye coordination and motor skills. They can also help with language, too! When speaking about the pieces, direct your niece or nephew with descriptive words, like "straight-edged pieces" and "corner pieces." This will help develop spatial relations.

❋ **Bath time:** Bath time is one of the best times for learning! Children learn the science of cause and effect, when things float and when they sink.

❋ **Fill 'er up!** Ever notice how little kids love to pour things from one cup to another, especially when they are mixing various colors of juice? This is science, Auntie! They are learning about spatial relations and physics. All they need is a lab coat and they're all set. You, on the other hand, will probably need a few paper towels on hand for the inevitable spills.

❋ Acting out: Want to develop children's creativity and self-confidence? Help them put on a little show. Give them each roles to play, and get them started on a story line. (A fairy princess is looking for her magic wand . . . ) They'll learn how to weave a story together.

## Head Games

For practically every aspect of a child's mental and social development, there's a game that'll help hone essential skills. Here's how you can play your way to an independent, conscientious, well-adjusted niece or nephew.

| TO PROMOTE . . . | TRY PLAYING . . . |
| --- | --- |
| Focus and concentration | I Spy, musical chairs, or Red Light/Green Light |
| Memory skills | Simon Says |
| Self-control | Simon Says, Do the Opposite |
| Communication | Tongue twisters |
| Spatial understanding | Hide-and-seek |

Source: Ellen Galinsky, *Mind in the Making: The Seven Essential Life Skills Every Child Needs*

## Let's Head Outside!

In his book *Last Child in the Woods: Saving Our Children from Nature-Deficit Disorder*, Richard Louv talks about the importance of bringing a child back to nature. In fact, he argues that time outdoors is a must, as much as things like homework or after-school activities like ballet lessons are. The learning, discovery, and fresh air counterbalance the overscheduled stress that many children, even small children, feel. In fact, studies indicate that children with attention-deficit/hyperactivity disorder (ADHD) are more likely to do better in green settings than industrial ones. Nature enables them to be more focused.

You can introduce more nature into your nieces' and nephews' lives as soon as they're old enough for outings without Mom. Describe what they're seeing aloud, or turn over a log to investigate the worms and bugs underneath. In autumn, pick up fallen leaves for pretty craftmaking materials.

Just about everything you encounter in nature is worthy of a conversation. What's that sound? What kind of insects are those? Talk about trees, birds, and flowers. To a child, grown-ups are expected to know the names of every single living creature, so bring along your smartphone or a nature book for on-the-spot research in case you're stumped.

Another great place to learn is the beach. Filling up pails of sand, building castles, showing how some things float while others sink. The sun dries our wet bathing suits. Wet sand is muddy and sticky, but dry sand is loose.

## Be Cool, Read a Book!

Once your niece or nephew is old enough to focus on a book's illustrations, describe the pictures as you point to them. Even if the book doesn't have words (which it probably won't at this stage), a baby learns language and vocabulary by hearing you speak, so describe everything on the page in detail. Label the colors and shapes, and describe spatial relations and emotions:

* A round, yellow sun

* Tall, green grass

* Little, pink bunny rabbit

* Smiling, happy baby

If the picture shows a number of similar things, count them aloud by pointing at each one: How many duckies are there? One, two, three!

Books designed for babies often include textures, shapes, and colors. Point out similar shapes, colors, and textures in your niece's or nephew's nursery. Is a favorite plush animal "soft"? The crib is smooth. The baby's brush is shiny.

As you read a niece's or nephew's favorites again and again, point out new things each time:

* The round yellow sun is high in the sky.

* The tall green grass is in front of the house.

* The little pink bunny rabbit is hopping.

* The smiling, happy baby has brown hair and he's wearing a white diaper with duckies on it.

# I Want My AunTieV!

Lots of quality television programming is available for children these days. And many shows are cleverly produced so that a parent or auntie can enjoy the show on a different level than the kids do. *Sesame Street* often includes parodies of adult-appropriate shows like *Mad Men.* And *Yo Gabba Gabba!* features celeb guests and musical numbers chosen for adults to appreciate. Children love when you watch with them (which is called coviewing), and you can take this opportunity to continue talking about the lesson or moral of the show once it's over.

Still, there's a lot of controversy over so-called educational videos. In October 2009, Disney recalled its *Baby Einstein* videos because of claims on the packaging stating that the videos were educational; the Federal Trade Commission refuted that claim. And in the book *Anytime Playdate: Inside the Preschool Entertainment Boom,* author Dade Hayes cites a 2007 study from the *Journal of Pediatrics* that said that children between the ages of eight and sixteen months who watched an hour of video a day on a regular basis "resulted in them understanding six to eight fewer vocabulary words." On the other hand, reading or telling stories actually added two to three words.

It's no surprise, then, that in 1999, as videos for babies were becoming a behemoth industry, the American Academy of Pediatrics recommended no video, TV, or any screen-presented media viewing for babies age two and under.

For kids ages two to five, preschooler-tailored videos and TV shows are more accepted. Shows like *Sesame Street* are known to help kids develop their cognitive skills, while others, like Nickelodeon's *Dora the Explorer* and the newer *Ni-hao Kai-lan,* focus on what the network calls "emotional curriculum."

## Rhyme, Read, Repeat!

> Because babies have so many new things to absorb every day, they find comfort in the sameness of their favorite books, games, rhymes, and stories. Repeating something over and over is also how a child gains a sense of mastery and control, which is very satisfying and empowering.

If you're starting to get tired of the same book over and over, try reading in different voices, or letting your niece or nephew finish the sentences she or he knows by heart.

(A Savvy Auntie tip: Did you know that the children's classic *Goodnight Moon* features a hidden mouse on each page? Same goes for *Goodnight Gorilla,* except it's a hidden balloon. I thought we'd keep it interesting for you, Auntie.)

# Social and Emotional Development

So we've got our nieces and nephews well on their way to strong cognitive development. But what about their social and emotional development? How will they learn how to treat other people, to become independent and autonomous, and to understand social cues?

According to a report from the National Research Council of the Institute of Medicine entitled *From Neurons to Neighborhoods,* "responsive, nurturing relationships with parents and caregivers [that's you, Auntie!] are the key predictors of 'healthy intellectual and emotional development.'" This means that just hanging out and spending qualauntie time with your little nieces and nephews is shaping them into wonderful human beings.

Now, it's true that a baby's first order of emotional attachment is to his or her mother. Babies even just a day or two old can tell the difference between Mom's scent and anybody else's scent. (Our smart nieces and nephews know where their next meal is coming from!) However, Mom isn't the only one who can offer them a sense of emotional contentment and well-being. All caregivers can do that.

In the 1950s, Dr. Harry Harlow at the University of Wisconsin conducted a now-famous study testing how a monkey finds its mother. In the test, monkeys were exposed to two different "mothers," one a dummy constructed out of wire mesh and embedded with a baby bottle, its nipple sticking out. The other "mother" was dressed in a soft terrycloth fabric but didn't have a bottle. Time and time again, the monkeys chose the warm, huggable mother. Unless they were hungry—

## *Auntie Up!* How Do You Make Learning Fun?

*The passenger seat in my car was dubbed "the learning chair," because every time one of my nephews sits in it, he learns something before he gets out. My third-youngest nephew always looks forward to it, and we've shared some deep and some outright silly conversations.*

—Nicole Joseph, Sacramento, CA

*I taught my niece her name through a song. Even before she could talk, I would sing, "Karla, K-A-R-L-A!" As she got older, she could sing along. Now, she's three and she can spell her name backwards and forwards.*

—Regina Townsend, Chicago, IL

*My oldest nephew is three. Before he goes to bed he'll sit down with me and we'll play a flashcard game on my iPhone that he likes. My rule is, he has to say the name of the object or number on a card correctly before he can change the picture.*

—Tanya Torrance, Brewer, ME

*My nephew is seven and we're writing a story together, a chapter each!*

—Jen Jacobs, New South Wales, Australia

then they'd suck on the bottle offered by the wire-mesh monkey and then return immediately to the terrycloth monkey.

The study concluded that nurturing is a key factor in attachment, even more so than nourishment. This doesn't mean that moms are not the ones babies attach to the most, as mothers provide both nourishment and nurturing. But it does show that babies are able to have attachments to people other than their mothers.

# Growing Emotionally

To best help the social and emotional development of her nieces and nephews, an auntie should change up her strategies as they age. According to the Zero to Three organization, here's how to do so during babies' first, second, and third years:

## The Theme:

0 to 12 months: Responsive care

12 to 24 months: Self-control and limits

24 to 36 months: Empathy and self-expression

## What to Do:

### 0-12 MONTHS:

Pinpoint what they're pointing to. Take time to try to understand and figure out what they want. Show you care about their frustrations.

Cheer on accomplishments: He reached for the ball! She turned over all by herself! Kids love encouragement, which teaches them to try harder.

Be affectionate and nurturing. Sounds easy–except when the baby is colicky and fussy. Stick it out so the baby feels loved through thick and thin.

Stick to routines. Mom and Dad probably have your niece or nephew on a pretty good schedule; follow it so the child feels safe. At your place, sing familiar songs, play with familiar toys, and call their other caregivers by the names the baby knows.

### 12-24 MONTHS:

Be firm but gentle. Let toddlers know that they can't do whatever they want.

Talk about their feelings: "Abby is sad that she can't hold the grown-up knife." Stating the obvious shows you understand where they're coming from.

Show them appropriate ways to show feelings. Remember that song, "If you're happy and you know it?" It's designed just for this reason!

Help them cope. If a nephew doesn't want to go for a walk when it's his routine time to get some fresh air, tell him you understand, but a rule is a rule. Give him something else to focus on and soon he will begin to soothe himself, a very important skill.

Teach by example. When things don't go your way, stay calm, count to ten, and show the kids that not everything is the end of the world.

24-36 MONTHS:

Help them hug it out. Encourage them to give a hug to a hurting friend or even a grandparent who isn't feeling well.

Teach emotional language. They're beginning to express their own feelings verbally. Encourage them to find words for their disappointment, sadness, and excitement.

Explore alternatives to hitting. Now is when unwanted behaviors such as hitting may start. Show them how using verbal skills is better.

Help them make friends. Enhance the value and importance of friendships by asking about their friends and all the people they spend quality time with.

Start explaining family relations. While they may not yet understand that you're their daddy's brother's wife, they will eventually. For now, at least, they'll understand that you're in the same circle of grown-ups they recognize, which will help them feel safe.

Teach social skills through picture books. This is a good idea if there's a particular skill they can use some extra coaching on. At this age, children can learn lessons as they relate to their own experience.

Why is attachment important, when the goal is for a niece or nephew to grow up to be an independent, autonomous human being? Early attachments have a very significant effect on how a child develops intellectually and emotionally. In fact, infants who had strong early attachments are better at make-believe play and problem solving once they reach two years of age. By four, they are able to show greater empathy for others and enjoy higher self-esteem.

Now, before you go out and buy a terrycloth robe for your next visit with your niece or nephew, remember that the behavior you're already doing—holding the baby, keeping the baby warm, feeding the baby a bottle, bathing the baby, massaging the baby, soothing the baby—are all ways you show the baby that she or he is beloved. When babies have a sense of security and comfort, they thrive.

*When babies have a sense of security and comfort, they thrive.*

# Auntie's in Charge

8

WHETHER FOR A FEW DAYS, or just a few hours, someday you may be put in charge, Auntie. Ah yes, I know the feeling. First there's a sense of elation ("I get him all to myself!"), but then the fear sets in ("I'm all by myself with him!"). No worries. I've put together *a few choice things to help you manage your day* in, or your day out, with your tiny tot. And I'm not just talking about how to take care of your niece or nephew, but yourself, too.

# Baby Nutrition

During the first four to six months of your niece's or nephew's life, the only items on the menu are breast milk and/or formula, which contain all the essential nutrients babies need at that age.

After that, when solid foods start getting introduced, most parents begin the baby on rice cereal, but it's a myth that it must be the first solid food ever given a baby. The American Academy of Pediatrics recommends that babies start off with iron-fortified foods, as babies of this age are known to become iron deficient; giving them either iron-enriched rice cereals (traditional) or pureed red meat (cutting-edge savvy) are two of the best things to offer them.

First foods can also include a pureed vegetable or fruit. Many babies love:

❋ **Applesauce**

❋ **Avocado**

❋ **Squash**

❋ **Sweet potatoes**

❋ **Carrots**

❋ **Bananas**

❋ **Peas**

❋ **Split peas (iron-fortified food!)**

❋ **Peaches**

❋ **Broccoli**

❋ **Green beans (iron-fortified food!)**

❋ **Pumpkin**

❋ **Mango**

❋ **Guava**

(For now, I suggest you skip berries, including strawberries, since some children might be allergic to them.)

# Homemade, Healthy Baby Food

Making a puree for your niece or nephew to dine on is really easy! Even if you swear you can't cook, I guarantee you can make baby food.

*Pureed Squash* (or pumpkin, sweet potato, carrot, etc.):

Microwave or steam squash until well cooked and soft.

Let it cool.

Puree in food processor.

Serve one to two tablespoons of squash to the baby.

Freeze the other gallon of squash, two tablespoons at a time, in freezer-safe Baggies. Or better yet, spoon pureed squash into ice cube trays for perfect portions. There, you just made dinner for a week!

*Frozen vegetables are even easier to make baby-ready.*

Defrost the vegetables and use an emulsion blender to puree. Serve.

Don't expect your niece or nephew to eat more than one or two teaspoons of solid food at a time to start with. Babies have a natural impulse to know when they are full, so when they start slapping the spoon, turning their heads, getting irritated, or crying, it's time to stop feeding.

While I recommend feeding your niece or nephew beef, chicken, lamb, or pork, I hope you won't feed them from your fast-food order. These meats contain many other ingredients the baby won't be ready for, including eggs, sodium, and added fat. Feed your baby niece or nephew unseasoned, well-cooked meats and make sure to puree them well so the baby can't choke on them.

Denise Fields and Dr. Ari Brown, coauthors of *Baby 411,* suggest feeding a baby just one food at a time during this first stage of solid food. This way, if an allergy appears, it'll be easy to figure out which food might be the culprit.

By the time the baby is nine months old, he or she is probably eating three solid meals a day (meals for them are counted in a few tablespoons) and three meals of breast milk or formula.

# Nutrition for Children

## Eating Through the Ages

How kids' eating habits and preferences change, ages 0-8:

| AGE RANGE | EATING HABITS |
|---|---|
| 6 months to 2 years | At this age, they'll eat just about anything |
| 2 to 4 years, give or take (can last longer) | During this phase, they often refuse to try new foods |
| 4 to 6 years | More willing to try new foods, but usually prefer mild, separately served foods |
| 7 or 8 years and up | Finally start to come around to new foods again! |

Source: Julie Negrin, M.S., www.julienegrin.com

## Fail-Safe Foods Kids Love!

When the kids are in their auntie's care, the "What do you want to eat?" conversation can drag on well past their appointed dinnertime. Lucky for us, Julie Negrin–kid nutritionist, cooking instructor, and author of *Easy Meals to Cook with Kids*–knows what kinds of foods never fail to please a crowd. (Bonus: They're all nutritious, too!)

| KIDS LOVE . . . | SO SERVE . . . |
|---|---|
| Finger foods | Wontons, pita chips |
| Colorfulness | Veggies like red peppers and carrots |
| Food that looks like trees (strange, but true!) | Broccoli, cauliflower, asparagus |
| Cheese sprinkled on top | All sorts of veggies and pasta |
| Patty shapes, small balls, foods in wrappers | Pot stickers |
| Anything mini | Minimuffins, miniburgers, etc. |
| Dips | Hummus, yogurt sauces, healthy ranch dressings (all good with veggies!) |
| Textures, although it varies; one kid might love smooth, another prefers chunky | Foods like guacamole in the texture you know they prefer |

## "Picky" Eaters

It can be a challenge when our little nieces and nephews are in our care and are not agreeable on any of the suggested food offerings. Some suggestions:

🍴 Ask your niece or nephew (in a light tone) to try just one bite and promise you'll be OK with it if she or he still doesn't like it. Always compliment them for giving it a try.

🍴 Reintroduce foods periodically. Many kids have to try a food several times before developing a taste for it, so keep on putting out those quesadillas–without forcing your niece or nephew to eat it.

🍴 Let your nieces and nephews see you enjoy a wide variety of foods, and say it aloud when you really love the (nutritious) food you're eating. Chances are, you'll make the kids curious to try it, too.

🍴 Try foods in different forms. A kid may not like a big piece of chicken drenched in sauce, but spoon off the sauce and cut up the chicken into bite-sized pieces and you might have a winner!

🍴 Don't allow kids to eat snacks right before meals!

🍴 Take focus off the food. Think of meals as quality talking and sharing time. It'll put less pressure on your niece or nephew to please you with a clean plate.

🍴 Give your niece or nephew a role in mealtime preparations, including menu selection. Try taking them to the grocery store and tell them you're going on a dinner "safari hunt."

🍴 Kids don't need to eat as much as adults, so take them at their word when they say they're finished.

🍴 When taking kids out to a nice restaurant, pretend you're all on an exotic vacation. Kids love immersing themselves in a story, so let your imaginations run wild!

🍴 It's fine if kids want to spit something out–but they must do so politely, into a napkin!

*So what's on today's menu, Auntie?*

Got the niece or nephew for an entire day? That's a lot of meals to be responsible for, Auntie! Here's an easy day's menu of nutritious kid-pleasers. Note that the goal is to get some protein in their bellies with each meal and snack, not just carbs. This'll help thwart whining and crying outbursts that sometimes result from a sugar crash. And of course, aim to keep 'em hydrated throughout the day.

❋ **Breakfast:** Oatmeal with cinnamon and raisins; yogurt/fruit/granola parfaits; last night's leftovers (if they want chicken for breakfast, give it to 'em!); buckwheat pancakes with fresh fruit

❋ **Lunch:** Grilled cheese sandwich with corn on the cob; tuna wraps; veggie burger

❋ **On-the-go snack:** Cut-up turkey hot dog; homemade veggie or fruit muffins; pita spears with hummus or yogurt dip; air-popped popcorn sprinkled with Parmesan; edamame; smoothies!

❋ **Dinner:** Breaded chicken or fish with homemade sweet potato fries; spinach lasagna with veggie tomato sauce; chili and cornbread; veggie quesadillas and guacamole

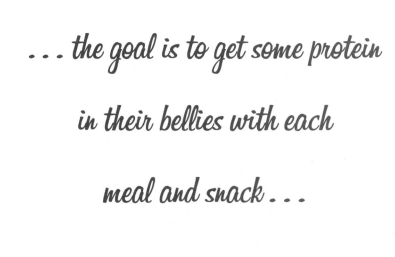

*. . . the goal is to get some protein in their bellies with each meal and snack . . .*

## Bath Time Safety Tips

When running the water, never let the child be in charge of the tap. Double-check the temperature before anybody gets in the tub.

Place everything you need within reach before placing your niece or nephew in the bath. Never, ever leave a child unattended in a bath even for a second. Remember, a child can drown in only two inches of water.

Most parents will recommend their tear-free, child-friendly shampoos and soaps. Don't substitute these with adult products.

Place a bathmat on the floor to avoid a slippery fall as your niece or nephew enters or exits a bathtub.

Keep all grown-up products like razors out of reach of children.

Most important, don't get distracted. If the phone rings, let it ring. If you must leave the bathroom, wrap the child in a towel and take him or her with you.

# Clean Kids

Bath time should be a wind-down to a child's chaotic day and an introduction to sleepy time. It should not feel like a chore for you, Auntie! In fact, it can be a calming highlight to your evening, too, with games that should entertain the both of you.

Bath toys are always a good idea. In a pinch, a child will find as much amusement in a Tupperware container or a clean yogurt cup.

Just as you love singing in the shower, your niece or nephew loves to sing in the tub! "Rubber Ducky" and "Splish Splash" are great bath time songs, but try being creative and singing something like "Itsy Bitsy Teeny Weeny Yellow Polka Dot Bikini"—and pretending you're at the beach.

# Clean House

Nieces and nephews love playtime with Auntie. Auntie loves a clean house. Combine the two into fun housecleaning games! Try these, recommended by Sittercity.com:

### Simon Says . . .

Mix picking-up chores into the game by giving commands like, "Simon says . . . everyone pick up one red toy! Simon says, put it in the toy chest!"

### Racing Music Mania

Gather the kids and your iPod. Pick your fave upbeat workout song and tell the kids that when the music starts, you'll all run around the room picking everything up. Give the game a "beat the clock" element and, for an added twist, toss in a "freeze" element by pausing the song once or twice.

### Pickup Parade

When there are several cluttered rooms, march through the house together picking up strewn-about items. For a mostly disposable mess, appoint one child in charge of marching along with a garbage bag.

Worried about messes? Never fear, smearphobes! Here's your A-to-Z guide to preventing, treating, and eradicating kid-created stains, as recommended by our resident Organized Auntie, Janice Simon, CPO.

**ASAP:** That's when you should treat stains! The fresher the stain, the more likely you can get it out.

**BABY CAR SEATS:** Wipe down the seat with warm water and dish soap. If the pull-out part of the seat is washable, run it through the washer following the manufacturer's directions. For a crumbly-food mishap, wipe off the sticky parts and vacuum out the crevices.

**CRAYONS AND MARKERS:** Use a Mr. Clean Magic Eraser to wipe off crayon and marker scrawls from hard surfaces. Remember that flat paint may come off the wall along with the stain, no matter how you clean it. Glossy paint makes cleanups easier.

**THE DRYER:** Never put a soiled garment in the dryer until you've done everything you can to remove the stain. Once the heat of the dryer gets to it, the stain will be set and likely to stay.

**ESSENTIAL STAIN-FIGHTING SUPPLIES:** Antibacterial wipes or cleansers, glass cleaner, Mr. Clean Magic Erasers, rug cleaner, dish soap, rubber gloves, a pretreating stain remover and paper towels.

**FOUNDATION, POWDER, BLUSH:** Rub heavy-duty detergent into the stain before washing.

**GUM:** When it's stuck on clothes, stick the garment in the freezer–or, if the niece or nephew is still wearing it, rub ice on the wad. Once the gum has hardened, it should be relatively easy to break or scrape off.

**HOMEMADE STAIN REMOVER:** An equal-parts mix of vinegar and water can be used in a pinch to clean and sanitize most stains.

"**I** WANNA DO IT!": **For elementary-age kids who want to pour their own milk or juice, give them a small pitcher or creamer to use, or keep a beverage container in the fridge that's got a spigot at the bottom, the kind kids can easily use without lifting.**

**J**UST **K**EEP SCRUBBING: **Mucho elbow grease is necessary to get out stains like Kool-Aid, juice, crayons, makeup, and nonpermanent markers, while walls, carpets, bedding, and clothing are the most difficult textiles and surfaces to render spic and span. But it can happen—especially if you attack the stains early.**

**L**IPSTICK, EYELINER, EYE SHADOW, MASCARA: **Treat with a stain stick, rub heavy-duty detergent into the stain, then rub with hot water until the stain is removed.**

**M**ATTRESSES: **Soak up accidents with damp paper towels. Keep dabbing until you don't see any more yellowness on the towels. Sprinkle Borax detergent on the affected area and scrub. Once the spot is dry, vacuum up the Borax.**

**N**AIL POLISH: **If it's on a rug, apply nail polish remover and blot several times. If it's on clothes, place the stain facedown on clean paper towels, apply remover to the back of the stain and keep replacing the towels as needed to soak up as much of the stain as possible, then launder as usual. (If the clothes are made of acetate, triacetate, or mod-acrylic fabrics, take them to the dry cleaner; nail polish remover will dissolve these textiles.) See also: Quick-drying nail polish.**

**O**IL-BASED STAINS (MAYO, SALAD DRESSING, BUTTER, LOTIONS, GREASE): **Rub with heavy-duty detergent before washing in warm to hot water.**

**P**ROTEIN-BASED STAINS (EGGS, BABY FOOD/FORMULA, BLOOD, MUD, GLUE, POOP, DAIRY): **To dislodge, soak the garment in cold water, then rub the stained area under cold, running water. (Hot water is a big no-no, as it can "cook" the stain into the fibers.) Launder with heavy-duty detergent.**

QUICK-DRYING NAIL POLISH: **It's the way to go when you and your niece have a nail-painting party. Another smart stain-preventing tip: Use a hair dryer on its coolest setting to set polish faster, and always put a towel down on the floor.**

RUGS: **Spray rug cleaner on the stain and let it set according to the manufacturer's directions. Blot several times, then vacuum.**

SIPPY CUPS: **Essential for cutting down on spills when you've got very young nieces and nephews. As they get a little older, switch to fun plastic glasses that come with lids and straws.**

TOWELS: **Drape bath-sized ones over nice upholstered chairs when the kids are eating. Afterward, you can just shake out the crumbs and wash the towels.**

URINE AND VOMIT: **When cleaning up bodily fluids from household surfaces (floors, etc.), use paper towels and bleach or another cleanser with antibacterial agents. (For bodily fluids on clothes, see Protein-based stains.)**

WATERPROOF MATTRESS COVERS: **A godsend when potty-training toddlers sleep over!**

GET X-TRA HELP **preventing stains by using products like Scotchguard to protect your couches and chairs and your car's fabric upholstery.**

SAY YES **to bibs and smocks during meals and craft times. Even if they've outgrown them or don't usually wear them at home, you're allowed to set the rules *chez vous,* Auntie.**

ZESTY, **fresh breath is only one thing toothpaste is good for. A savvy tip, courtesy of real-life Savvy Auntie Gail Friend in Laval, Quebec: "The best thing I've ever found to remove crayon and markers from my walls, tables–anything–is toothpaste. It really works, try it!"**

# Driving This Baby

Between the constant "Are we there yet?" questions and the boredom-induced backseat fights, driving with your nieces and nephews in the car can be as nerve-racking as when you first took your driver's test. But it doesn't have to be. Just follow these guidelines and it'll be smooth sailing—um, driving!

First off, *you* must follow certain rules in the car, too, Auntie! No cell-phone use whatsoever, and no distractions like a gossipy friend in the front seat or a loud stereo. You need to hear everything that's going on in that backseat. Speaking of the backseat, no trying to reach back there (to pick up a dropped toy or stop a fight) while driving. It's very dangerous.

Of course, always have the parents' permission before driving the children anywhere, and inform them of where you're going and when you plan to get back. Conversely, speak up to the parents if you're uncomfortable driving with the kids in rain, darkness, or other less-than-ideal conditions.

Get full instructions from parents on which child requires a safety seat and how to properly fasten it. Also, although your car comes with child safety and window locks, you may not know how to use them; consult your manual or ask a parent to help you figure it out (these safety devices are usually similar from car to car).

Don't allow your nieces and nephews to buckle themselves in, even if they claim they're big enough to do it on their own.

No kids in the front seat! The backseat has been proven to be the safest place for children under twelve, because the front-seat airbag is not designed for them and can actually pose a danger in the event of a crash.

Before heading out, let your niece and nephew select a few toys they'd like to bring along. Good choices are stuffed animals, coloring book and crayons, or a quiet toy like a Mini Magna Doodle. Try to dissuade them from bringing along noisy toys that might distract you or annoy the other kids in the car. Place the toys within the children's reach before departure.

Traveling with a diaper bag? Don't place it on the seat next to a child. He or she may get

## Sing-along with Savvy Auntie!

Need to distract or entertain your nieces and nephews? Sometimes nothing does the trick like an old-fashioned nursery rhyme. Go online to www .savvyauntie.com/l/songs to read the lyrics and listen to the melodies!

grabby and pull out a diaper wipe to gnaw on. Keep it on the floor of the front passenger seat.

Pack drinks and snacks for each child. When their mouths are full, they're quiet! Anything that's prepackaged as individual snacks (granola bars, juice boxes, cracker packets, etc.) works best to minimize arguments, since it's clear how much each child can have. Steer clear of foods that require utensils or foods that can be choking hazards, like baby carrots.

Kids who argue with one another should be separated. Ideally, give each one a window seat and let the scenery distract them.

Positive praise encourages good car behavior. You can even try awarding points for every five or ten minutes of good car behavior, then letting kids redeem their points later for something like an ice-cream pit stop on the way home.

Last but never least, Auntie, all nieces and nephews should go potty before getting in the car! (If they still wear diapers, make sure their bottoms pass the sniff test before departure.)

# Savvy Auntie 911

Just like the Boy Scouts, the Savvy Auntie's motto is: Be prepared! Should your niece or nephew ever have a medical emergency while in your care, planning ahead will prove a lifesaver. The following steps from Dr. Leigh Vinocur, an assistant clinical professor of emergency medicine at the University of Maryland School of Medicine, should be carried out before an auntie-supervised outing and really don't take much time at all.

Maintain a complete, updated medical history of all nieces and nephews (for infants, also have their birth history) along with a list of allergies they've got or medications they take. Keep copies at home, at work, in your car, in your wallet, and/or on your phone.

Program into your home and mobile phones the numbers for Poison Control, the closest hospital emergency room, and the children's pediatrician.

For longer stays or trips with Auntie, either Mom or Dad should sign a Consent to Treat form, granting you the right to authorize any emergency treatment or surgery for your nieces or nephews in their stead. (Download the forms at www.emergencycareforyou.org.)

Keep a kid-friendly emergency kit in your car for road trips with the nieces and nephews. Include a flashlight, bandages, antibacterial gel, wet wipes, several bottles of water, and an extra charger for your cell phone.

Ready for a big day out with a baby or toddler–but don't want to commit to carrying a dowdy diaper bag? You can turn any tasteful tote into a diaper bag on the inside. All that's required is that you categorize. Our Organized Auntie Janice Simon, CPO, to the rescue!

THE STUFF: **Food (Cheerios, baby carrots, etc.)**
TO STASH: **Put individual snacks into small Baggies, then tuck inside hardcover food containers.**

THE STUFF: **Drinks**
TO STASH: **Add a layer of protection to juice bags and boxes. Retailers like the Container Store have special products designed to prevent portable drinks from bursting open in your bag.**

THE STUFF: **Baby formula**
TO STASH: **Put dry formula powder into a baby bottle, then ask at an eatery for hot water when it's feeding time.**

THE STUFF: **Breast milk**
TO STASH: **Keep bottles prefilled with breast milk in the pocket of your bag normally used to hold a cell phone. Make sure you have a lid that snaps on top of the bottle to avoid leaks.**

*You can turn any tasteful tote into a diaper bag on the inside.*

THE STUFF: **Diapers and baby wipes**

TO STASH: **A diaper and travel-sized pack of baby wipes should slide easily into the zippered pouches of a tote or purse. (When traveling with a potty-training toddler, keep an extra pair of undies, and perhaps pants, too, in a plastic bag.)**

THE STUFF: **Baby powder and rash cream**

TO STASH: **Put travel-sized products into a snack-sized Baggie.**

THE STUFF: **Clothes**

TO STASH: **An extra onesie or fresh shirt can be rolled up, then slipped inside a plastic bag and tucked next to the diapers.**

THE STUFF: **First aid essentials**

TO STASH: **Put some antibacterial ointment, sunscreen, hand sanitizer, a few bandages, and some headache meds (for you!) into a Baggie or your makeup bag.**

# Savvy Auntiedotes for Common Ailments

Oh, no! Your niece or nephew is teething, but you forgot to pack a teething ring. Or it looks like she or he may be running a fever, but you're wary of giving medicine without permission from Mom or Dad.

Try one of these homemade, all-natural, doctor-endorsed remedies. Mom, Dad, Grandma, and everyone else will be amazed by your savviness!

| THE PROBLEM | THE AUNTIEDOTE | WHAT TO DO | HOW IT WORKS | POSSIBLE SIDE EFFECTS |
|---|---|---|---|---|
| Fever | Raw onion | Cut two chunks of raw onion, each sized to fit into one of your baby niece or nephew's socks. | Stick the onion in the socks so that the cut side is turned up toward baby's feet. Put baby's socks back on for a few hours. Onions contain anti-inflammatory properties. | Stinky baby! |
| Ear infection | Garlic oil | Warm up the oil and place a drop into the ear canal. Wait a minute, then drain. | Garlic is an antibiotic. | None! |
| Eczema, or any sort of itchy-skin situation | Vegetable shortening | Grease up the affected patches of skin a couple times a day. | Shortening's got emollients in it and is considered even more effective than petroleum jelly. | Slippery baby! |
| A cold | Vicks BabyRub—on the feet, not on the chest or around the nostrils | Rub well into the soles of the feet, put on socks, put baby down for nap. | Foot massage stimulates acupressure points that relieve coughing. Eucalyptus also helps with congestion. | None—but remember that this remedy isn't suitable for babies younger than three months. |
| Teething | Clove oil | Mix one drop of clove oil into one tablespoon olive oil and rub into gums. Repeat as needed every two hours or so. | Clove oil contains natural numbing properties. | Happy baby! |

Source: *Babytalk* magazine

# Choking Hazards

Savvy Aunties know that we need to be careful of what babies, toddlers, and small children put in their mouths. What may surprise you, though, is just how many different random (some even edible) items can prove to be choking hazards.

Here's a list of those you should know about. Of course, this is by no means the final say on what constitutes a choking hazard. Always be conscious of little things hanging around that little ones can get their hands on—especially when they come to visit you at home, Auntie.

## Food

**Note: Whatever type of food you're feeding a small child, make sure it's cut into pieces no larger than a half inch in diameter.**

❋ **Hot dogs (Cut them in half lengthwise, then into bite-sized pieces.)**

❋ **Grapes (Slit these in half lengthwise.)**

❋ **Hard candies and gummy candies**

❋ **Hard, raw veggies (like carrots)**

❋ **Popcorn**

❋ **Gum**

❋ **Peanut butter (Knowing there are no peanut allergies, spread thinly!)**

## Toys

**Note: If you're not sure whether the toy being played with is a safe one, see if it fits into a toilet paper roll. If it does, it's a choking hazard.**

❋ **Marbles**

❋ **Barbie shoes**

❋ **Jacks**

❋ **Game-board pieces**

❋ **LEGO and other small building pieces**

- ❋ Bits of crayon

- ❋ Tiny dolls

- ❋ Small balls

- ❋ Foam toys that can be bitten and swallowed

- ❋ Balloons (Mylar balloons are safer than rubber ones, as they pose less of a choking hazard.)

## Miscellaneous

- ❋ Rubber bands

- ❋ Safety pins

- ❋ Baby powder

- ❋ Pen caps

- ❋ Coins

- ❋ Bottle caps

- ❋ Rings, earrings, pins

- ❋ Hair elastics and clips

- ❋ Magnets

- ❋ Anything from the garbage can—put a lid on yours, Auntie!

# Discipline as a Savvy Auntie

I know your nieces and nephews are perfect, Auntie. But sometimes—and this can be our little secret—they act like, well, children. Which is why they need discipline, including discipline when they're in your care.

Now, you may be thinking, *But I'm the "cool auntie." I'm like their buddy, not their parent. That's why I love being the auntie—because I get to avoid being the disciplinarian.*

Sure, you can think that way. You can choose to conduct your auntie-ing in a rule-free, undisciplined zone and fool yourself into thinking that by treating your nieces and nephews as equals, you're practicing mutual respect and blah blah blah.

Here's what will happen: your nieces and nephews will learn to walk all over you. You will find yourself kowtowing to the dictatorial whims of a two-year-old. You may even really frustrate the parents who are putting so much effort into turning out well-mannered, well-adjusted kids.

So you're not going to do that. You're going to get on board with the discipline stuff. Do we understand each other? Good. Now please observe the following:

Learn their parents' discipline style. If the children are given time-outs when they misbehave, be consistent and give them time-outs for the same length of time as they get from their parents.

When the children are in your care, you're the boss. If you say it's time for them to put on their coats, then the coats are going on their bodies. If it's time to leave the bookstore, it's time to leave the bookstore. If you told one of them not to throw a toy, he gets a time-out if he throws the toy. Remember, if they know they can manipulate you, they will. So don't give in, no matter how many tears.

The "terrible twos," which really last from about eighteen months to three years old, are a notorious time when a child is trying to exercise his or her autonomy, which generally presents itself as a screaming fit. If you say "right," they may say "left" just to show you who's boss. In that case: *you're* the boss.

Safety comes first. If they run into the street without warning, make sure they understand that you are upset and why. Get down to their level and look them straight in the eyes and tell them why what they did was dangerous. Make them repeat it back to you so you know they've heard you and understand.

# Temper Tauntrums

As savvy as we are, sometimes our precious little nieces and nephews cause us to . . . Just. Totally. Lose. It. When that happens, it is our job to keep ourselves in check and self-administer whatever sort of time-out we need. Here's what you do.

Think positively. Losing your cool, immediately followed by telling yourself how terrible you are for losing your cool, will only leave you feeling more vulnerable and thus more likely to again lose your cool. Instead, tell yourself that you're not the only person in the world who's gone through this and that you can handle the situation.

Acknowledge your meltdown. Explain to your niece or nephew in calm tones why you just freaked out, why it was wrong, and what you'll try to do differently next time. If nothing else, this will help turn your tauntrum into a teachable moment.

Never hit. I know this goes without saying, but I'm saying it anyway. Never, ever hit a child.

Return the kids to their rightful owner. This is absolutely a time when, as the nonparent, you've got the "advauntage." But do talk things out with Mom or Dad, too. They've probably got some good tips for how you can cope better next time, and everybody needs support now and then.

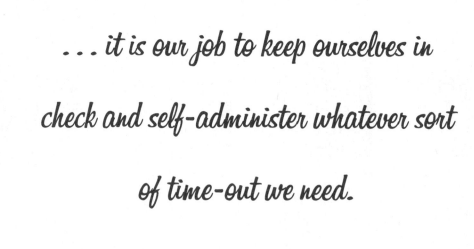

*. . . it is our job to keep ourselves in check and self-administer whatever sort of time-out we need.*

# Money and Legal Savvy

AT THE BEGINNING OF THIS book, I described the power of the PANK (Professional Aunt No Kids). Never before have women enjoyed as much financial independence and influence as we do right now. What this means, dear Auntie, is that you—whether you're a Single Auntie, Married Auntie, Mommy Auntie, or anything in between—are *more likely than ever to enjoy a unique financial outlook* that enables you to help pamper, plan, and provide for all the important people in your life. That includes you, your immediate kin, your nieces and nephews, and even the kids of your own you may one day have.

Many Savvy Aunties want to provide for our loved ones so much that birthday presents or amazing vacations aren't enough. We want to financially contribute in manners so profound, they can't be packaged in mere wrapping paper. A Savvy Auntie may want to earmark some of her savings so her nieces and nephews can benefit from a top-notch education, or experience a special rite-of-passage trip abroad, or enjoy a fabulous wedding they'll remember forever, or make a down payment on their first home.

Such plans and possibilities are all very exciting to think about, but in life we also must make sure that we plan for the worst. Sometimes bad things happen to good people. Savvy Aunties are always prepared, even for the worst, and it's often up to an Auntie to step in and provide care or guardianship to our precious nieces and nephews when necessary. This chapter gives you the tools to do it all—to make sure the necessary safeties are in place for those tricky situations, and then to plan proactively for all the wonderful things that await you in your future auntiehood.

# Money for Nothing! How to Give Tax-Free Cash Gifts

Did you know that you can give each niece and nephew (as well as each parent) up to $13,000 per calendar year, without the recipient owing any taxes on it? Monetary gifts from one individual to another under $13,000 (a figure that was raised from $12,000 a few years ago) are considered tax shielded. You don't need to declare the gift in any way, and the recipient's bank won't report it or ask questions about it when it's deposited, either. This is a wonderful way to help pay for private schooling, tutors, music lessons, sports camps, and so on. It also allows you to help out in a pinch (braces, unexpected medical bills, unforeseen schooling costs) when needed.

That amount is also excluded from the taxable part of your estate . . . when you die, which won't be happening any time soon, so no need to worry about that! But, says Galia Gichon, personal-finance expert and founder of DowntoEarthFinance.com, "It can help a person tremendously that has a good bit of money and is focused on estate planning."

## A Few More Words of Common Cents

Review your saving plans for yourself and your nieces and nephews annually, like a doctor's checkup. This way you can ensure that your money is working for you and them in the best ways possible.

If your niece or nephew ever incurs an unexpected medical expense that is beyond her or his parents' financial means, you can give a gift of more than 7 percent of your annual income with a tax break the year you gave the money. You may also take funds out of your 401(k) without penalty for this reason.

And of course, please speak with a financial adviser before making any significant changes to your long-term savings plans. Tax laws and investment laws are known to change!

# The 411 on 529s, Coverdell, and Other Educational Savings Plans

If there's one thing most aunties probably want to help pay for, it's college. And if there's one thing the government seems intent on making very confusing for you, it's helping pay for college. The

| SAVINGS VEHICLE | WHO CAN CONTRIBUTE? | WHAT CAN IT BE USED FOR? |
| --- | --- | --- |
| 529 college savings plan (named after its numbered section in the tax code) | Anyone | Tuition, housing, books, fees, equipment, etc., at any accredited U.S. college or university (and some foreign ones) |
| 529 prepaid tuition plan | Anyone | Educational expenses at in-state public universities |

good news is, there are more ways to save for secondary and postsecondary education than ever before—and several of them can be contributed to by any friend or family member.

| TAX BENEFITS | OTHER BENEFITS | POSSIBLE DRAWBACKS |
| --- | --- | --- |
| Investment gains aren't taxed, so as long as money's taken out for qualified educational expenses (tuition, etc.), distributions from the account are tax-exempt. Choosing the plan offered by your own state often comes with additional tax benefits. | Can be transferred to another niece/nephew, or even back to yourself. (Culinary school, Auntie?) Can be used toward graduate school. While every state offers at least one 529 plan, you don't have to choose the one from the state you live in, the state your niece/ nephew lives in, or even the state of her/his college. In other words, you can shop around (and even move to another state's plan if you later find one you like better). | If the money is taken out for nonqualified expenses, it's taxed and also subjected to a 10 percent penalty. Since a person can have only one 529 plan to his/her name, the parents will probably be in charge of the account, and you'll just contribute to it. Many have contribution maximums. |
| Not as many as college savings plans | You're basically "prepaying" for a future college student's tuition at today's prices! The Independent 529 Plan, sponsored by about three hundred private/public schools nationwide, offers greater flexibility. Unlike college savings plans, there are no market investment risks; prepaid tuition plans are state-backed and guaranteed. | You must use the plan offered by the state where your niece or nephew resides, and she or he must attend that state's public universities, limiting future educational choices (although there are refund options). Not all prepaid tuition plans cover room and board, books, etc. |

| SAVINGS VEHICLE | WHO CAN CONTRIBUTE? | WHAT CAN IT BE USED FOR? |
|---|---|---|
| Coverdell ESA (education savings account) | Anyone who meets an income-limitation standard (see Possible Drawbacks) | Elementary, secondary, or postsecondary educational expenses |
| UGMA (Uniform Gift to Minor Act) | Anyone | Anything! College, travel, a car, etc. |
| UPromise.com, a program that saves a percentage of money spent at restaurants, shopping online, using your credit card, using your grocery store card, etc. | Anyone | Investing in an already-established 529 plan, investing in a high-yield savings account, paying down student debt, or you can just request a check for any other expenses |

| TAX BENEFITS | OTHER BENEFITS | POSSIBLE DRAWBACKS |
|---|---|---|
| Same as 529s | Ideal for private-school students | If you earn more than $110,000 (or $220,000 if you file a joint return), you're not allowed to contribute. Like 529s, there are taxes and penalties if the money's taken out for nonqualified expenses. Comes with contribution limits. |
| The money is tax deferred and comes out in the child's tax bracket, which is low compared to a salary-making adult's | No maximum contribution amount. First $13,000 contributed per adult per year is shielded by gift tax laws. Allows for transfer of stocks, bonds, annuities, life insurance policies, etc., from investor to recipient, not just cash. | Money can't be accessed until child turns eighteen or twenty-one (depending on the state). The investor (you) gets no legal say in how or when the recipient spends the money. Money cannot be retrieved by the investor once it's deposited. |
| None | Lots of freedom in how you spend your savings (since it's not a government-created program). Lets you save without having to make room for it in your budget. | Do you really need more incentives to shop till you you drop, Auntie? |

# Guardianship: Becoming a ParAunt

If your minor-aged nieces' and nephews' parents are unable to take care of them—for reasons that might include illness, abuse, incarceration, or death—then a legally appointed guardian, usually a family member or close friend, takes over as the ParAunt. For everyone involved, it's best that all the legal work needed to line up the guardian is squared away in advance. In fact, it should be done as soon as possible after the baby is born.

Of course, this is a subject nobody ever really wants to talk about, and the parents of a newborn have plenty of other important tasks keeping them busy. Don't be afraid to raise the issue matter-of-factly, if only to make sure that taking care of legal guardianship gets put on their to-do-soon list. If you don't feel comfortable being up front about it, Alexis Martin Neely, founder and CEO of the Family Wealth Planning Institute, suggests saying something like, "Hey, sis, I was just reading in the paper about a family that hadn't named guardians for their kids and then something happened to the parents and there was a big family fight. Have you given this issue any thought for Janie and Joey?"

If the decision is made to make you the legal guardian, the parents should definitely have a will drawn up naming you as their children's legal guardian and designating that you receive money and other things needed to raise them. However, a will alone is not the best idea. Wills need to be interpreted by a court through a process called probate. This process can be lengthy and expensive in some states—and in all states, it's a public process, which might not make things as easy as possible for the family.

The only foolproof way to avoid probate is to make sure that all the parents' assets are in a living trust—to which you, the legal guardian, are named as its trustee and beneficiary. (Still, they should also have a will, especially when there are things not covered in the trust. It's best to make sure that the beneficiaries are the same in the will and the trust or things may get held up in the court system. Cover your bases, Auntie!)

A living trust is like a box of all assets: houses, bank accounts, brokerage accounts, and business interests. If all of these assets had to go through probate, it could take years before you could access them. The trust is an agreement between the grantor of the trust (your nieces' and nephews' parents, also called the creator, trustor, settler, trustmaker—all the same name for the one

# Who's the Best Legal Guardian?

As you probably know, you may not be the only possible choice for a legal guardian that your nieces' and nephews' parents have. And I think the savviest thing to do in this situation is to help those parents objectively decide who's best for the job. After all, the nieces' and nephews' well-being is the most important thing.

I asked family legal expert Darlynn Morgan for her advice on the subject.

First, parents should make the longest list they can of everyone they know who might make a good guardian, including all those who would provide a better home for the children than the foster care system would provide. (However, this doesn't mean candidates should be excluded for financial reasons. A well-counseled estate plan will ensure that there are enough financial resources available for the care of your nieces and nephews.)

Although most parents will say that their single most important consideration is that their children are raised by someone who loves them, the truth is that many other factors will play a role in what sort of upbringing the children may have without the parents. What sort of religious environment (or lack thereof) will they be raised in? Who else would live with the ParAunt and the kids? Would the kids have to move away from where they've grown up in order to live with a particular ParAunt?

To keep both sides of the family close and involved—not just with the legal process, but with the nieces and nephews on a personal level—some parents may consider naming members from one side of the family as guardians to care for the children, but members from the other side as trustees to manage the assets.

What if you haven't made the final cut, Auntie? In that case, ask how you can help the guardians and get those privileges put in writing. For example, the parents may stipulate that you have certain visitation rights with your nieces and nephews. Take care of yourself so that you can take care of your nieces and nephews should it ever come to that.

who holds the assets) and the trustee of the trust (you). The grantor gives assets to the trustee for the benefit of the beneficiary (your nieces and nephews). So basically, as long as the parents are alive, they are the grantor, trustee, and beneficiary all rolled into one. They haven't given up any control by putting their assets into a trust.

Should something happen to your nieces' and nephews' parents, then you, as trustee, would work with a personal lawyer to gain access to the trust's assets and either hold them for the beneficiaries in a continuing trust, or transfer them to the beneficiaries and terminate the trust. This process is generally quicker and less expensive than probate and always totally private.

Finally, even more important than all this documentation, your family will benefit greatly from having a strong relationship with a personal lawyer who will guide you and your nieces' and nephews' parents toward smart decisions. Trusts and wills are both important, but your family deserves the comfort of a trusted adviser who knows all of you, and what's important to all of you.

*. . . your family deserves the comfort of a trusted adviser who knows all of you . . .*

# Celebrating You, Auntie!

**10**

WHEN YOU BECOME AN AUNTIE, there's an extra swing in your step, a twinkle in your eye, and the sky is blue even on a rainy day. You never knew there could be a love like this. *Few things in life are worth celebrating more than a niece or nephew entering the world.*

However, one thing you should always remember to celebrate, dear Auntie, is you. I say this knowing that sometimes—especially for Single Aunties and/or aunties with no kids of their own—it will feel as if the rest of the world has decided to do the opposite, devaluing our fabulousness and overlooking all that we offer our loved ones, little and big. Chances are you've been on the tail end of a few choice zingers that call your marital status (or lack thereof) into question. Maybe you've had to fight hard at work for some flextime or a personal leave of absence, while parents seemingly get time off willy-nilly. (And doesn't that feel doubly unfair to those of us who'd actually really *like* to be mothers?) Don't even get me started on those family get-togethers where you're still expected to sit at the kids' table. Or the injustices, both familial and societal, that every LesbiAunt has endured from time to time.

With such pressures and stereotypes upon us, a Savvy Auntie sometimes needs her own special set of tools to help her on her journey, all of which you'll find in this chapter, along with abundant reasons why you should continue celebrating *you*. No matter what's on your mind—whether you're worried about your fertility or you're ready to just kick up your heels and get down to party—consider these pages for Savvy Aunties only: strictly *auntre-nous*.

# The DebutAunt Ball

The rite of passage into auntiehood is a big one, and what better way to commemorate the occasion than a DebutAunt Ball!

Unlike a baby shower or a niece's or nephew's birthday party, a DebutAunt Ball isn't about the parents or the children, although perhaps you'll invite them, and it isn't about giving gifts, although I do have great ideas for gifting a sister or friend who's about to become a DebutAunt. The DebutAunt Ball is simply a way to mark this next big step and awesome responsibility in your life, Auntie, or in the lives of other Savvy Aunties who follow in your footsteps. (In addition to throwing your own party, I definitely recommend hosting a DebutAunt Ball for a friend or family member when her time comes. It's like paying your Savvy Auntiehood forward!)

However you want to celebrate is entirely up to you. If you want to invite the baby's mama, that's great! However, some mothers may not like that you're observing this moment as your own. We're sure you know your relationship with your niece's or nephew's parents well enough to decide whether or not you should keep your party on the down low.

To make your DebutAunt Ball quite the to-do, here are a few quick and easy party-planning tips that'll get you started.

## DECOR

Decorate in pinks, blues, or whatever colors best represent your newborn niece or nephew. Also think about fresh accent hues: tangerine, light aqua, pear green. When in doubt, just go with Savvy Auntie pink! (Hint: It's the color of this book.)

Hang a WELCOME TO THE WORLD sign with your niece's or nephew's name on it.

Pick a flower and make it your theme. (If your niece has a flower for a name—Rose, Lily, Daisy, etc.—then the choice is easy!) In years to come, give your niece a bouquet of that flower every year on her birthday, or do the same for your nephew's mother on his birthday. And of course, treat yourself to a dozen for every auntieversary!

## REFRESHMENTS

Bake or buy cupcakes or cookies frosted in your party's chosen color. Expecting twins? Make two batches of everything in complementing colors!

Serve a DebutAunt highball! As every Savvy GourmAunt knows, a highball is any kind of simple cocktail made with a liquor and a nonalcoholic mixer (soda, juice, etc.) served on the rocks. Our DebutAunt highball recipe is a pared-down, highball-style take on the Pink Lady, a cocktail from the 1930s that was in vogue among society ladies of the time. I like the idea of taking something old-fashioned and putting a modern spin on it, as that's what Savvy Aunties are all about. (Also, it's pink!)

Fill a highball glass with ice.

Add a shot of your favorite gin.

Fill glass with lemonade. (Homemade is best!)

Add a splash of grenadine and stir vigorously.

Garnish with a maraschino cherry.

## GIFTS

Again, gift giving isn't essential for a DebutAunt Ball, but it might be nice for all your guests to pitch in on one top-of-the-line item, like a digital camera for a DebutAunt who can use some memory-capturing technology, or a laptop webcam so that a Long-Distance Auntie can video-conference with her nieces and nephews. A brand-name, slouchy hobo bag is also a great gift, as it makes for a fashionable diaper-bag substitute for those special days alone with the baby.

### AUNTIVITIES

Pass around a cute, blank journal and ask each Savvy Auntie to jot down what she's learned since her own DebutAunt days.

Share photos of one another's nieces and nephews.

Using a doll or stuffed animal, and this book as a guide, practice changing diapers, swaddling, and burping.

Quiz time! Who's the Savviest Auntie of them all? Have a little fun with the following SAT: Savvy Auntitude Test on page 206! (As a prize for the winner, how about a copy of this book?)

### THE DEBUTAUNT DINNER

If hosting a DebutAunt Ball isn't your thing, consider planning a fun night out with your closest friends at your favorite restaurant. I recommend ordering a bottle of rosé prosecco (pink bubbly, perfect for Savvy Aunties!) and eating dessert first—as a Savvy Auntie in the making, it's time to get comfy with breaking the conventional rules and roles. And to remind yourself to see the world through a child's eyes!

### THE DEBUTAUNT DAY OF BEAUTY

Daytime a better time? Go with a few Savvy Auntie friends to get manis and pedis. (Blue polish for a nephew, Savvy Auntie pink for a niece?)

# Isn't It Romauntic? Five Reasons a Savvy Auntie Makes a Great Date

1. She's a fun font of endless conversation. Of course, a Savvy Auntie loves gushing about the great kids in her life. But obviously, those kids aren't the only things she's passionate about or eager to discuss. A Savvy Auntie knows when to keep kid talk in check; on a first date, she'll just share one of her iPhone photo albums labeled "Cuties." (The other twelve slide shows can come later!)

2. She's down with divorced dads. Being totally cool and comfy around kids makes the Savvy Auntie especially appealing to the single father—a guy who's often pretty mature, serious about relationships, and in search of a woman who knows how to handle a young heart.

3. Auntie's savviness is always "on." On an ice-cream date, she effortlessly enters a game of peekaboo with the toddler waiting for strawberry with rainbow sprinkles behind them. When headed to brunch, she doesn't scoff at a fleet of strollers blocking the restaurant's doorway. She'll always toss a runaway ball back to its tiny owner. Her date gets to see her easygoing confidence in all she does.

4. She remembers to ask him about the kids in his life. Just like aunties, uncles come in all forms; your date may not have a sibling with kids, but he's probably got a buddy or two who does. It's also likely that he doesn't get many opportunities to talk about his unclehood (the way you do with your auntourage), so he appreciates having someone who wants to hear about it.

5. She trusts the young ones' judgment. Guys think of puppies as chick magnets; Savvy Aunties know that their nieces and nephews make great guy barometers! After a few dates, she may invite a new beau on an outing with her nieces and nephews. They'll know whether or not he's truly Savvy Uncle material!

# The Savvy Auntitude Test! (SAT)

1. **What is baby cruising?**

    a. When babies hold on to furniture, railings, and so on, as they begin to take their first steps

    b. When a five-year-old prodigy is enrolled in first grade, since he or she would "cruise" through kindergarten anyway

    c. When using a hands-free baby-toting device, like a sling or backpack, to make errand running much easier

    d. When Tom Cruise marries a much younger woman

2. **What is a baby burrito?**

    a. A popular choice of infant food in Acapulco

    b. A style of diaper

    c. The result of wrapping a baby snugly in a receiving blanket

    d. Parenting slang for a baby who's fed a lot of rice

3. **Which of the following is a key component of Dr. William Sears's parenting methods?**

    a. Shopping with baby for low, low prices on appliances

    b. Feeding a baby at least five times a day

    c. Parents and babies sharing the same bed

    d. Using flash cards to communicate with a baby eighteen months or younger

4. **Where do water births usually take place?**

    a. In the freshwater body of Mom's choice

    b. Special birthing tub

    c. That depends on an Aquarius mom's astrological chart

    d. In Seattle

5. **The pregnancy-related blood sugar condition that affects about 5 percent of expectant women starting around Week 24 of their pregnancies is known as . . .**

    a. Glucositis

    b. Gestational diabetes

    c. Fetal stroke

    d. Ice cream and pickles syndrome

6. **Why is a college savings account referred to as a 529?**

    a. Because that's how much one textbook is going to cost in eighteen years

    b. The interest on it is fixed at 5.29 percent

    c. It's named after the line of the U.S. tax code in which it appears

    d. The maximum amount a nonparent can contribute is $529,000

7. **What's Stokke?**

    a. A Scandinavian stork

    b. A parenting guru

    c. It stands for Sleepy Time Often Kills Kids' Energy

    d. A brand of baby gear

8. **According to the Toy Industry Association, all of the following are appropriate toys for children under six months of age EXCEPT:**

    a. Wading pools

    b. Interlocking rings

    c. Activity gyms

    d. Rattles

9. **When making dinner for your niece or nephew, what's a good way to childproof the cooking area?**

    a. Switch to a raw-food diet

    b. Heat foods in the microwave to avoid open flames

    c. Order in!

    d. Turn pot handles in toward the center of the stove top

10. **What are baby bumpers?**

    a. Pads that prevent a sleeping baby from rolling over

    b. Pads that prevent a baby from getting hurt against the sides of a crib

    c. Pads that keep a baby secure inside a pram or stroller

    d. Clumsy babies

Answers: 1.a 2.c 3.c 4.b 5.b 6.c 7.d 8.a 9.d 10.b

# Questions and Aunties:
## How to Handle the Awkward Stuff Nieces and Nephews Ask

When your home life doesn't exactly resemble that of your nieces and nephews, questions about Auntie will inevitably arise. Why are there no kids in your house, Auntie? How come you're not married? How come you live with another lady?

To help you answer like a champ, I've rounded up some women I trust who know a thing or two about going down these delicate roads. Take their time-tested advice and these awkward Q&As should transpire smoothly. (No upsetting of Mom or Dad necessary!)

Q: How come you don't have a husband?

A: I have a surefire response for this. Tell your nieces and nephews, "Because if I got married to a man, he'd become your uncle, right?" It may take them a moment to understand this, but once they do, explain to them, "So I can't just marry any old guy. He'd have to be really special to be YOUR uncle, right?" They'll likely agree with this more readily: "Yeah!" Next say, "Well, I'm still looking for someone special enough to be your uncle. But when I do get married, will you be my flower girls and ring bearers?" "YEAH!" Then quickly change the subject.

–Esther Kustanowitz, a Savvy Auntie in Los Angeles, CA

Q: I heard someone say you're a lesbian. What's a lesbian?

A: It's hard to address this question without thinking about whether the child's parents want them to know the answer. People usually don't say stuff like, "Don't tell the kids until they're older," but they do sometimes think it, or hope desperately that you won't talk about it, like a "Don't Ask, Don't Tell" mentality. If the parents have said that they don't want you discussing it (and this is their prerogative), ask them what you should say instead and use their words–unless you strongly disagree, and then you'll all need to find words you can agree on.

People never wonder how to tell a child what a heterosexual is. Usually, an adult just explains that men and women get married and have babies. So what you can do is define lesbian for them in terms of family. Tell them that two people who love each other–a man and a woman, a woman and a woman, or a man and a man–are what make a family. As for the sexuality aspect, unless someone has already told them that it's not OK, kids aren't going to ask why two women are holding hands.

–Susan Pinkwater, MSW

Q: How come you don't come over with Uncle Ted anymore?

A: When there's a separation or divorce, you should first ask your niece's or nephew's parents if they want to tell the child about it in their own way. But inevitably, a child will direct questions toward you. Take age into account. The limited understanding of a three-year-old means his or her questions will be very ego-driven: Does this mean I won't get presents from you anymore? Will you still come visit? In contrast, a teenager or preteen might take a philosophical look at the situation: What does it take to make a relationship work? Why do some relationships end?

If possible, you and your partner should speak to the kids together. Agree not to blame each other in front of them. Start with simple statements, such as, "We've been having grown-up problems. We've tried to work them out and now we've decided to live separately. That means we will see you separately, too." You can talk about being sad and even a little scared, since things will be different than before. Tell them that you both love them, which will never, ever change. And if you can make a definite plan to see them in the near future, that can prove reassuring.

–Natalie Robinson Garfield, psychotherapist

# Benefits of Being a Savvy Auntie (and Not a Mom)

No matter what the reason for your child-free life—choice, circumstance, whatever—your fabulous life has got some truly fauntastic advantages.

* **Savvy Aunties are thinner.** A study conducted in Australia found that the moms they observed gained twenty pounds over ten years, while nonmoms "only" gained ten. (Hey, we'll take what we can get!)

* **Savvy Aunties have more friends.** For people with no children, the average number of close friends is 4.7, according to a recent study–a number that gradually declines to just 3.5 close friends for parents with three kids.

* **You can be more spontaneous.** Feel like getting a manicure after work? Or saying yes to a drink with a coworker? Sure.

* **You're saving a lot of money.** I mean a *lot* of money. According to the U.S. Department of Agriculture, it costs $222,360 to raise a child to the age of eighteen–and that doesn't include college tuition.

* **Cornell University sociologists found** that mothers, even those that chose to return to work, suffered a substantial wage penalty compared with women without children.

* **You'll never find Cheerios in the backseat of your car.** Speaking of cars, you can choose the one that fits your lifestyle and yours alone.

* **You'll have a happier marriage.** The *Journal of Marriage and Family* reviewed one hundred studies and concluded that married couples with children had unhappier relationships than married couples without children.

* **You can travel wherever you want, whenever you want.** Bon voyage, Auntie!

## Your "Hormoney" Checkup Checklist

Food's not the only factor that impacts hormonal balance. The good news is, many other possible problems can easily be checked out by your physician or ob-gyn. Alisa Vitti, HHC, AADP, founder of FLOliving.com and the FLO Living Center in New York, recommends making an appointment if you're experiencing a prolonged or acute case of any of the following:

Chronic fatigue

Depression or anxiety

Constipation, bloating, or diarrhea

Absent or irregular menstrual cycles

Acne, oily skin, or skin discolorations

PMS

Unexplainable weight gain

## Becoming a Mom Someday and Getting in "Hormoney" with Your Body

Whether getting pregnant is part of your five-year plan or something you jotted down on today's to-do list, there are steps you can take right now that will help enhance your fertility and prolong the onset of perimenopause, the transitional stage before menopause when ovulation may cease (even if menstruation continues) and that generally takes place during your forties but can begin for some in their thirties. Many of these fertility boosters are simple lifestyle changes with lots of beneficial side effects—namely, all-around improved health! Practically all of them boil down to the same thing: being hormonally balanced. There are dozens of hormones coursing through your

# *Auntie Up!* Got a Good Savvy Comeback?

A Savvy Auntie can always depend on the rudeness of strangers–or siblings, in-laws, friends of friends, sometimes even our own parents–when it comes to queries about her ovaries. Are they open for business? Are they just on strike? What are they waiting for?

Take heart, Savvy Auntie–and heed these always-witty, often-candid, and occasionally heartfelt comebacks that other Savvy Aunties just like you have come up with to ward off unwelcomed inquisitions.

*I have been blessed to be able to love so many others' children—if I had my own, I would constantly feel guilty for sharing too much of my love.*

—Lynsi Brierly, Knoxville, TN

*My sister has enough kids for the both of us! As far as the grandchildren quota is concerned, it's taken all the pressure off me.*

—Maggie May, San Diego, CA

*Why have kids when you can borrow your niece and nephew? It's always better to spoil 'em, fill 'em with sweets, and send 'em home.*

—India Williams, Washington, DC

*My children are of the four-legged kind. When I'm ready for the two-legged, I'll let you know.*

—Heidi Spintig, Holiday, FL

*I'm not a vomit and poopy-diaper kind of girl.*

—Tami Bronstein, Highland Park, NJ

*I usually tell people, "We forgot!"*

—Kitty Gellanis, Fairfax, VA

*I simply say, "I'm too selfish." Harsh, but ends the pressure immediately!*

—Kristine Pfeiffer, Hoboken, NJ

*I say, "I'm the aunt. I have nine nieces and nephews, and I'm part of the village they need to grow up. Our village does need an idiot, though."*

—Janice Simon, Houston, TX

*I'm not ready to share my husband yet; I like getting all of his attention and care.*

—Bobbie Hyun, Macon, GA

*I simply say, "Being a mom wasn't in the cards for me, but being the fun, crazy aunt was!"*

—Rosy Villa, Los Angeles, CA

*I ask them why, if a little ten-year-old girl says she wants to have a baby one day, they respect her decision, but they feel completely comfortable questioning mine.*

—Marcia Bryant, Cleveland, OH

*Because kids are precious and I didn't want to screw one up like so many kids today are. They usually shut up after that.*

—Susan Plunkett, Tempe, AZ

*I never wanted children. When I was a kid, people used to tell me my opinion would change when I got older; I hated that. I'm forty-three now, and people still tell me I'll change my mind eventually. I usually answer with "When? When I'm sixty?"*

—Amy Gugig, New York, NY

*Missing out? I won't argue that point, but it's hard to miss what you never wanted in the first place.*

—Diane Bishop Stevens, Old Saybrook, CT

body, and the over- or underproduction of any one of them can impair your reproductive health, as I learned when I consulted with Alisa Vitti, HHC, AADP, founder of FLOliving.com and the FLO Living Center in New York.

Let's start with diet, which can have a profound impact on pregnancy whether you want to be with child next week or sometime in the next decade. Yes, there are "fertility-friendly foods" (see the list opposite) you can and should add to your diet, but what's equally important is *how* you eat.

Are you a superbusy Savvy Auntie who often skips meals, or who subsists on nothing but salads, coffee, and late-afternoon chocolate fixes? Do you strive to maintain a zero-fat diet, banishing good fats along with the bad? Thanks to all the hours you spend at the office, are you a vending-machine junkie (and hey, it's not your fault the thing's only stocked with cookies and snack cakes)? These habits will work to destabilize your blood-sugar levels and may even lead to an onset of hypoglycemia. Throw your system out of whack often enough and your adrenal glands may decrease their production of DHEA—a hormone so critical to fertility that doctors often prescribe it (in synthetic versions) to women suffering from diminished ovarian reserve.

Of course, how you eat (and exercise, too) has a lot to do with whether you might be over- or underweight. Neither is ideal for conception. Insufficient body fat contributes to anovulation (a.k.a. not ovulating) and if you're not ovulating, you're not going to get pregnant. On the other side of the equation, too much body fat can likewise disrupt your cycle, as well as make it difficult to figure out when you're ovulating and lead to an overproduction of estrogen. Again, all hormonal imbalances are detrimental to conception. That includes insulin, which as we all know, can go off kilter thanks to packaged foods made from refined flours and sugars.

This sounds like advice you've read in countless magazines, I'm sure. But the reason you keep seeing it over and over is simply because it's true. Think of it this way: If your body's not feeling like it's in tip-top shape, why would it want to take on the added burden of another body growing inside it? When it comes to conception, "help me help you" is what I bet your body wants you to know.

# Fertility-Friendly Foods

Lean beef, brown rice, potatoes, halibut: Rich in vitamin $B_6$, which is believed to lengthen a woman's luteal phase, the time between ovulation and menstruation ideal for conceiving. Brown rice and other whole grains also help regulate blood-sugar levels.

Full-fat dairy: For real! A recent Harvard study found that eating full-fat dairy products—including *ice cream!*—decreased subjects' risk of anovulation, while consuming low-fat dairy may actually *increase* infertility. The only catch: You can't down so much chocolate mint chip that you wind up gaining weight, since being overweight never helps fertility. Many experts counsel keeping your full-fat dairy helpings to one serving a day.

Ginger: According to traditional Chinese medicine, ginger helps to dry up internal dampness in the reproductive channels.

Beans, lentils, black-eyed peas: These foods are filled with folate (a.k.a. folic acid or vitamin $B_9$), which contributes to egg production, placenta formation, and successful implanting of a fertilized egg in the lining of the uterus. Folate intake is also a key way to prevent birth defects once you are pregnant.

Olive oil, avocado, nuts, seeds: These "healthy-fat" foods provide the essential fatty acids that are critical for supporting overall hormonal health.

Turmeric: Improves the vascular health of your ovaries and packs a powerful antioxidant punch, keeping your genetic material fresh.

Leafy greens like bok choy, kale, cabbage, arugula, and chard: Chockablock with calcium and magnesium, which work in tandem to support the fallopian tubes as they do their job of making sperm and egg meet, then implanting the fertilized egg in the uterus.

While it's always preferable to "eat your vitamins," taking supplements to increase fertility is a beneficial and widely accepted practice. B-complex and $D_3$ daily supplements are just two you should ask your doctor about.

## The Celiac Connection

You've probably heard of gluten-free diets. They sound like the latest fad but are actually of prime health importance to those with celiac disease, an autoimmune disorder that results in an inability to tolerate gliaden, a protein found primarily in wheat. Alisa Vitti tells me that she's seeing more and more of a link between gluten sensitivity and hormonal imbalance. In fact, infertile women are ten times more likely to have celiac disease, while 39 percent of women with celiac disease suffer from amenorrhea (absent menstrual cycles).

Celiac disease symptoms can vary greatly and some people with celiac disease show no symptoms at all. However, the most common ones are fatigue and intestinal distress. If you're concerned, talk it over with your doctor; he or she can perform a celiac panel, a series of blood tests that will check for celiac disease.

# Fertility-Preserving Dos, Don'ts, and Duhs

Following are just a few more words of wisdom I wanted to pass along.

DO: Take up yoga or dancing—two activities that flush cortisol and adrenal hormones from the body. If you want to get in good prepregnancy shape, this is a better choice than, say, hard-core training for a triathlon, which can actually exacerbate adrenal fatigue, says Alisa Vitti, HHC, AADP.

DON'T: Burn the candle at both ends. Take a night off from your social life as needed and always get your seven to eight hours of ZZZs. Overextending yourself reduces your immunity, which can also lead to increased internal inflammation.

DUH: Whenever you're not in a monogamous relationship, use condoms and get screened for STDs annually (or as needed, in case a condom breaks). Chlamydia and gonorrhea are just two STDs that, if left undetected, can lead to infertility.

DO: Go easy on the alcohol. There are conflicting opinions out there about how much a woman can or should imbibe when trying to conceive—if at all. Alcohol does increase the concentration of c-reactive proteins (CRP) in the body, which act as inflammatories. Completely giving up alcohol is up to you, but a drink once or twice a week will likely do no harm. (As for several drinks several nights a week . . . you know you shouldn't do that even when you're not trying to conceive, right?)

DON'T: Hang around Debbie Downers. When it comes to your body's biology, renowned women's health expert Dr. Christiane Northrup firmly believes that "you are what you think." And since what you think can be strongly influenced by others, scale back from seeing those friends (well-meaning though they may be) who take a pessimistic view of future pregnancy.

DUH: No drugs!

DO: Get what you deserve in bed. (Yes, Auntie, even when that means, ahem, giving it to yourself.) Vitti and other experts like her believe that orgasms can actually improve a woman's fertility. True, the research on this is not 100 percent conclusive—but can you think of a better reason for a little bedroom fun?

DON'T: Smoke. Don't smoke! DON'T SMOKE!

DUH: Thirty-five is just a number—not a law. Same goes for forty. Same goes for forty-five. Says Dr. Northrup, "I've seen so many patients over age forty who found the love of their lives, got pregnant, and delivered a healthy baby. The fertility industry does women a disservice making them believe otherwise."

# Savvy Auntiehood: Practically Perfect in Every Way

A lot of presumptions exist about what life is like for Savvy Aunties. And most of these myths are overdue for a good debunking, especially since they get in the way of the real truth: that Savvy Auntiehood is an incredibly joyous endeavor and a very fulfilling life.

For example, many of us Savvy Aunties do not have children of our own, which can mean being voluntarily or involuntarily childless, child-free for now, circumstantially infertile, or that we're

## AUNTIEPEDIA:
## WORDS FOR WOMEN WITHOUT CHILDREN

CHILDLESS: **Has neither borne nor adopted children, no matter what the reason.**

CHILD-FREE, VOLUNTARILY CHILDLESS, OR CHILDLESS BY CHOICE: **Chooses not to have children.**

INFERTILE: **Has not been able to conceive.**

CIRCUMSTANTIALLY INFERTILE: **Hasn't become a mother because certain prerequisites for doing so—finding a long-term romantic partner, for example—haven't fallen into place yet. Also called involuntarily childless or social infertility.**

FENCE-SITTERS: **Still unsure whether or not they want children.**

CHILD-FREE FOR NOW: **When they feel ready, these currently childless women will reconsider having children.**

DINK (DUAL INCOME NO KIDS): **A professional couple that does not have children.**

PANK (PROFESSIONAL AUNT NO KIDS): **The segment of women who do not have children of their own, no matter the circumstances or reasons.**

CHILD-FULL: **A life filled with joy from all kinds of children, whether or not one's own.**

SAVVY AUNTIE: **A woman who loves a child- or children-not-her-own, regardless of whether or not she also has her own children.**

still fence-sitting on the whole kids thing. No matter which one we are, a common misconception is that because we don't have children or are delaying having children, we must somehow feel less happy than people who are parents. Yet in a June 2010 *Washington Post* article, Amy Pienta, associate resident scientist of the Inter-University Consortium for Political and Social Research at the University of Michigan, stated that research shows how "childless women are as happy as women who had children at typical ages. They are not any more depressed; their psychological well-being is just as high."

Simply being who we are is far too often regarded as "different"—which I put in quotes to emphasize how some people say that word as if being different is a bad thing. Here's a great rebuttal: in his book *The Forgotten Kin: Aunts and Uncles*, author Robert M. Milardo, PhD, a professor of family relations at the University of Maine, writes, "Parents and nonparents, homosexuals and heterosexuals are valued as aunts and uncles in part because the social conventions that define aunting and uncling simply permit, and sometimes even encourage unconventionality." The notion that our uniqueness is precisely what makes us such a highly valuable member of the American Family Village is one of the loveliest ideas I've ever heard.

And happily, the attitudes of others toward us Savvy Aunties are improving. The General Social Survey reports that in 2002, 59 percent of adults disagreed that people without children "lead empty lives," an increase from the only 39 percent of adults who disagreed with that statement in 1988.

What if we wind up never having kids? Then our golden years will be just as golden. A 2007 study by the University of Florida found that women with kids and women without kids report equal levels of psychological well-being well into their fifties. Far more important than procreating, the study found, were several factors, including education, career, financial earnings, quality of relationships with family and friends, being healthy, and having a husband or partner. Now doesn't that laundry list of laudable qualities remind you of someone you know, Auntie?

Auntiehood in and of itself has a profound and positive effect on our own personal development. Says Milardo, "The relationships aunts and uncles establish can provide personal satisfaction, opportunities for the development of lifelong friendships, a connection to family and community, a sense of place located in the convoy of generations and the opportunity to enact generative themes." In other words, auntiehood gives meaning to our lives today, and whether we wind up single, partnered, or parenting, we give meaning to the generations to come.

While we Savvy Aunties are renowned for all that we give our nieces and nephews, selflessly and unconditionally, it is their gift to us—in allowing us to be aunties just by their very existence—that is the most generous gift of all.

# Book Club Party

Grab your auntourage, Auntie! It's time to plan a Savvy Auntie Book Club Party!

Here's how I recommend you host your very own Savvy Auntie Book Club Party:

❋ **Make sure each Savvy Auntie has a copy of *Savvy Auntie*.**

❋ **Each auntie should wear a name tag with her "Auntie" name.**

❋ **I highly recommend you serve Savvy Auntinis (recipe on page 227) and ask each member of your auntourage to bring a niece's or nephew's favorite dessert (how fun!).**

Using *Savvy Auntie* as a basis for conversation, help one another get more savvy! You can cover one chapter each time the auntourage meets, and/or add your own topics based on current news. (Check out SavvyAuntie.com for the most recent studies, up-to-date headlines, and other current topics.)

# Discussion Points

### Chapter 1: An Intro to Savvy Aunthood

1. How do you pronounce aunt or auntie? What is your auntie name? What language is it? How do your little nieces and nephews pronounce it?

2. I outlined nine Savvy Auntie principles. Do you agree with them? Did I miss an important principle?

### Chapter 2: Welcome to the Auntourage

1. I describe the different kinds of auntie types. Go around the room and share what type of auntie type you think you are. Are you an ABR, ABC, LDA? A combination of many auntie types? Did I miss an important auntie type?

2. I know you're Savvy, Auntie! But what kind of Savvy are you? Check out our list on page 29 and share what kind of Savvy Auntie you are. Or have the auntourage make their call!

3. Celeb aunties! Who's your favorite and why?

### Chapter 3: The Aunticipation!

1. How did you first find out you were going to be an auntie for the first time? Go around the room and share your story.

2. While we may all be ecstatic to find out we're going to be aunties (again!), learning that someone close to us is expecting a child may make us think about our own fertility if we want children of our own. How did the news feel?

3. Anyone have an interesting story about when the mom-to-be was expecting? How did you help the parents prepare for the baby?

4. Baby names! We love baby names! Tell the room about your nieces' and nephews' names and why they were chosen. Do you love the names? Find them "interesting"?

## Chapter 4: Congrauntulations! You're an Auntie!

1.  Describe what it was like when you first saw your niece or nephew.

2.  What did you buy your little niece or nephew when she or he was born? Did you get anything for the parents?

3.  What's your Savvy Auntitude? Do you have skills? What are you best at? Diaper changing? Bathing? Swaddling? How do you get a baby niece or nephew to calm down? Do you have tips to share with the auntourage?

4.  Auntie-oops! What was your first big mistake with the baby?

5.  There are a lot of different parenting methods. What type of method do your nieces' and nephews' parents rely on? Do you agree with the method? What would you do differently?

6.  They grow up so fast! What's a baby milestone you can't wait to share? When did the baby first say your name?

## Chapter 5: Festivaunts

1.  Did you take part in organizing your niece's or nephew's first birthday party? Was there a theme? What did you learn for the next time?

2.  Holidays can be a wonderful time to spend with your nieces and nephews, but if you're an LDA (Long-Distance Auntie), it might be harder to be with them. What do you do to stay connected?

3.  How do you celebrate the holidays with your nieces and nephews? Have you instituted any traditions you can share?

## Chapter 6: Gift-Giving Savvy: Fauntastic Toys, Clothes, and Books

1.  What are the best clothes and toys you've bought your nieces and nephews?

2.  What are their favorite books? What books do you recommend?

3.  What are you favorite stores or online shops for gifts for your nieces and nephews?

4.  Do you consider yourself a spoiler? Do you ever get in "trouble" for giving the children too much?

### Chapter 7: A Is for Auntie

1. What do you do to help your nieces and nephews learn as you play with them?

2. What are your favorite games to play with them?

3. What are your favorite songs to sing with them? Have you made up a song for them?

### Chapter 8: Auntie's in Charge

1. Do you end up taking care of your nieces and nephews often?

2. What are your tips for entertaining them?

3. What was the craziest thing that ever happened when they were in your care?

4. What are the rules when you're in charge? Are there any rules? How do they differ from their parents' rules?

5. Do you have any special discipline strategies that work with your nieces and nephews?

6. What are you nieces' and nephews' favorite foods? Is there something special you prepare for them?

7. What are the kids' favorite snacks? Is there a healthful alternative you've introduced them to?

8. Are your nieces and nephews overeaters or undereaters? What tips have you found work best?

### Chapter 9: Money and Legal Savvy

1. Have you invested in a college savings plan or any other type of savings plan for your niece or nephew?

2. Have you thought about making your nieces and nephews your beneficiaries? What steps have you taken to make that happen?

3. Are you your nieces' or nephews' legal guardian should anything happen to their parents? If they have not yet named a legal guardian, would you want that role? Have you discussed it with their parents?

4. Are you your nieces' and nephews' ParAunt? Have you become their guardian? What's that transition been like?

## Chapter 10: Celebrating You, Auntie!

1. Do you think aunties make good dates? How's your romauntic life? Are you looking for a partner who might be a father to your children one day?

2. Do you want children of your own?

3. What are you doing to preserve your fertility?

4. What are the best things about being an auntie and not a mom?

5. What are your favorite comebacks for why you don't have kids (yet)?

6. What's more important to you: finding love or having a child of your own?

7. What is the best part about being a Savvy Auntie?

# Savvy Auntini Recipe

In ice-filled cocktail shaker, combine:

One shot (2 oz) vodka

1 oz white crème de cacao

1 oz light cream

Splash of grenadine

Shake, pour into a chilled martini glass, and garnish with a sprig of mint.

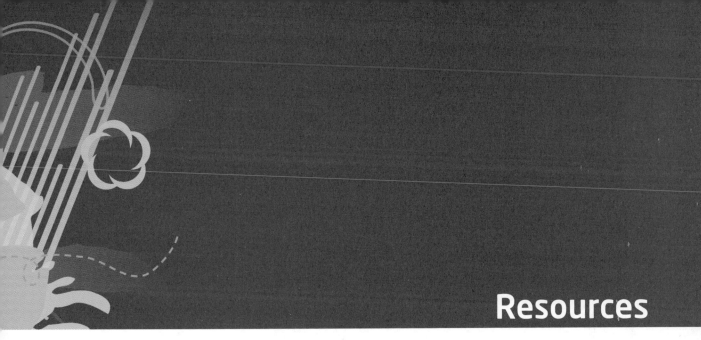

# Resources

One of the best parts of writing this book for all you Savvy Aunties out there was discovering so many valuable online resources, interviewing so many incredible experts, and reading so many other great books! In this section, you'll find information on books, websites, and other resources for you, in case you want to delve deeper into a specific topic on your own.

## Authors and Experts

Natalie Angier, *Woman: An Intimate Geography* (Anchor, 2000)

Stephanie Baffone, LPCMH, NCC
   Stephaniebaffone.com
   @sbaffone

Madelyn Cain, *The Childless Revolution: What It Means to Be Childless Today* (Perseus Publishing, 2001)

Nicki Defago, *Childfree and Loving It!* (Vision, 2005)

Dr. Bella DePaulo, *Singled Out: How Singles Are Stereotyped, Stigmatized, and Ignored, and Still Live Happily Ever After* (St. Martin's Press, 2006)
   Belladepaulo.com

Denise Fields and Dr. Ari Brown, *Baby 411: Clear Answers & Smart Advice for Your Baby's First Year* (Windsor Peak Press, 2010)

> Thebaby411.com
>
> @baby411

———. *Toddler 411: Clear Answers & Smart Advice for Your Toddler* (Windsor Peak Press, 2009)

Ellen Galinsky, *Mind in the Making: The Seven Essential Life Skills Every Child Needs* (Harper, 2010)

Natalie Robinson Garfield, *The Sense Connection: Discovering How Your Five Senses Determine Your Effectiveness as a Person, Partner, and Parent* (iUniverse, 2009)

> Thesenseconnection.wordpress.com
>
> @nrgimages

Galia Gichon and Anne Smith, *My Money Matters: Tools to Build Peace of Mind and Long-Term Wealth* (Plain White Press, 2008)

> Downtoearthfinance.com
>
> @simplymoney

Elizabeth Gilbert, *Committed: A Skeptic Makes Peace with Marriage* (Viking Adult, 2010)

> Elizabeth also coined the term "Auntie Brigade." You can read my interview with her here: Savvyauntie.com/l/auntiebrigade
>
> ElizabethGilbert.com

Heidi Green, Heidi Green Photography

> Heidigreen.com
>
> @heidigreenphoto

Dr. Miriam Greene, *Sexual Health with Dr. Miriam Greene*

> Dr. Greene hosts this satellite radio show on Sirius Channel 114 and XM Channel 119: Sirius.com/doctorradio

Dade Hayes, *Anytime Playdate: Inside the Preschool Entertainment Boom* (Free Press, 2008)

Kathy Hirsh-Pasek and Roberta Michnick Golinkoff, *Einstein Never Used Flash Cards: How Our Children Really Learn—And Why They Need to Play More and Memorize Less* (Rodale Books, 2003)

Lisa Kothari, *Dear Peppers and Pollywogs: What Experts Want to Know on Planning Their Kids' Parties* (Peppers and Pollywogs Press, 2007)

> Peppersandpollywogs.com
> @lisakothari
> Facebook.com/pepperspollywogs

Richard Louv, *Last Child in the Woods: Saving Our Children from Nature-Deficit Disorder,* updated and expanded ed. (Algonquin Books, 2008)

Jeannine Mercurio, AuntieScopes

> Savvyauntie.com/l/auntiescopes

Dr. Robert M. Milardo, *The Forgotten Kin: Aunts and Uncles* (Cambridge University Press, 2009)

Alexis Martin Neely, *Wear Clean Underwear!: A Fast, Fun, Friendly and Essential Guide to Legal Planning for Busy Parents* (Morgan James Publishing, 2008)

> Alexismartinneely.com
> Familywealthmatters.com
> Kidsprotectionplan.com
> @alexisneely
> Facebook.com/playbigwithalexis

Julie Negrin, *Easy Meals to Cook with Kids* (Authorhouse.com, 2010)

> Julienegrin.com
> @julienegrin
> Facebook.com/mykitchennutrition

Dr. Christiane Northrup, *Women's Bodies, Women's Wisdom: Creating Physical and Emotional Health and Healing,* rev. ed. (Bantam, 2010)

> Drnorthrup.com
> @drchrisnorthrup
> Facebook.com/drchristianenorthrup

Ana Schechter, Ana Photo Photography

> Anaphoto.net
> Rootingfortinyvictories.com
> @anaphoto

Janice M. Simon, MA, CPO
> Theclutterprincess.com
> @janicesimon

Lyss Stern, founder of Divalysscious Moms
> Divalyssciousmoms.com
> @divamoms
> Lyss is also editor in chief, *Observer Playground* magazine: observer.com/playground

Dr. Rosemarie Truglio, VP Education and Research, Sesame Street
> Sesamestreet.org
> @sesamestreet
> Facebook.com/sesamestreet

Alisa Vitti, HHC, AA DP, founder
> Floliving.com

Laura Wattenberg, *The Baby Name Wizard* (Broadway, 2005)
> Babynamewizard.com
> Namecandy.com
> @babynamewizard
> @namecandy

## Online Resources

Babytalk magazine
> Babytalk.com

The Bump
> Thebump.com
> @thebump
> Facebook.com/thebump

Centers for Disease Control National Vital Statistic Reports (Final Data 2006)
> Cdc.gov/nchs/data/nvsr/nvsr57/nvsr57_07.pdf

Child Product Recalls (not including toys)
> Cpsc.gov/cpscpub/prerel/category/child.html

College Savings Plans by State
Savingforcollege.com
Collegesavings.org

Fertility of American Women 2008
Census.gov/prod/2008pubs/p20-558.pdf

Fertility websites
Fertilityauthority.com
Fertilityties.com
Thefertilityadvocate.com
Eastcoastfertility.com

Jewish Treats
Jewishtreats.org
@jewishtweets
Facebook.com/jewishtreats

The Lollipop Book Club
Lollipopbookclub.com
@lollipopbook

Mothers of Supertwins (the most popular resource for moms of supertwins)
Mostonline.org

PANKs: Professional Aunts No Kids
Savvyauntie.com/l/PANK

Resolve: The National Infertility Association
Resolve.org

Sesame Street
Sesamestreet.org
@sesamestreet
Facebook.com/sesamestreet

Sittercity

    Sittercity.com

    @sittercity

    Facebook.com/sittercity

Toy Industry Association

    Toyinfo.org

    @toyindustryassn

    Facebook.com/pages/toy-industry-association/93917064185

Zero to Three

    Zerotothree.org

## ABOUT MELANIE NOTKIN

Melanie Notkin is America's premier Savvy Auntie, empowering the nearly 50 percent of American women who are not moms to celebrate all they do for the children in their lives, while living their own lives to the fullest. She launched SavvyAuntie.com, the first online community for aunts and godmothers, in the summer of 2008; and in the summer of 2009, she launched Auntie's Day, the first national holiday to honor aunts and aunthood.

Melanie identified this influential segment of women, which she has dubbed PANKs (Professional Aunts No Kids), when she herself became an aunt. As a child lifestyle expert and tastemaker, Auntie Melanie has been featured numerous times on TV, radio, and online. SavvyAuntie.com was a 2009 Webby Award nominee for Best Family/Parenting site and was a Springwise.com Top 10 Lifestyle and Leisure Business Idea, 2008.

She is a Savvy Auntie and Auntie by Relation (ABR) to her nephew and nieces, the loves of her life. She is also an Auntie by Choice (ABC) to all of her friends' kids, who come in a very close second. Melanie resides in New York where she is surrounded by the very best the city has to offer.

You can find more Savvy Auntie at:

SavvyAuntie.com

MelanieNotkin.com

Twitter.com/SavvyAuntie

Facebook.com/SavvyAuntie

Youtube.com/SavvyAuntie

You can e-mail Melanie at Book@SavvyAuntie.com

# Index